A ids and
R esearch
T ools in
A ncient
N ear
E astern
S tudies

3

DANIEL C. SNELL

A WORKBOOK OF CUNEIFORM SIGNS

Revised 1982 Edition

AIDS AND RESEARCH TOOLS IN ANCIENT NEAR EASTERN STUDIES

Editor: Giorgio Buccellati

This cuneiform workbook gives a course of programmed instruction teaching the 110 most frequently used signs. It teaches the standard Neo-Assyrian sign forms and gives the student practice both in passive and active recognition of the signs. The signs are divided into eight sections, and each section ends with a quiz reviewing all signs presented; appendices provide an alphabetic list of values taught and a list of the signs. The *Workbook* is designed for home study by students in beginning Akkadian classes and provides a practical introduction to the cuneiform writing system. It may be used in conjunction with R. Labat's *Manuel d'Epigraphie akkadienne* as well as the readings planned by the instructor.

Sixth Printing 2008

ISBN: 0-89003-058-8

Issued under the auspices of IIMAS – The International Institute for Mesopotamian Area Studies

Contents

Introduction

Passive recognition is the usual goal of learning cuneiform signs in Akkadian instruction in Europe and America. A method encouraging active use of the signs is presented here on the grounds that an active knowledge of the signs will stay longer with the student.

The idea for this workbook is taken from Japanese Kana Workbook by P. G. O'Neill (Palo Alto and Tokyo: Kodansha International, 1967), which I have found successful in teaching the Japanese syllabary. (1)

The signs to be taught were chosen on the basis of their frequency in Giorgio Buccellati's list of sign frequencies (2) in non-royal letters in F. R. Kraus' Altbabylonische Briefe. (3) I am much obliged to Buccellati and his students for this material and to him and Piotr Michalowski for other helpful comments. All signs presented here occur as more than 0.10% of that corpus. For simplicity only the more frequently attested values of the signs are taught here.

I have used Buccellati's list of sign frequencies because it is the only one available to me, but it does introduce a logical contradiction into this work: though the sign forms are Neo-Assyrian, the signs taught are chosen on the basis of a corpus from 1000 years earlier. This contradiction can be accepted on the grounds that the Old Babylonian period is in many ways regarded as a classical period both by the ancients who looked back to it for norms in various areas and also by moderns who frequently use its relatively simple syllabary and texts for beginning instruction in Akkadian. One might argue that it would have been valuable to present the signs in their Old Babylonian forms, but that would make it difficult for the beginner to consult the various manuals that are organized according to Neo-Assyrian sign forms.

This work is not, obviously, an original contribution to syllabary study, but merely a systematic way of learning some of the more frequently used signs. Ideally it should be used as part of a course with a teacher who will ask students to learn sign values and signs that will be of use to them in the readings planned. It should be used in conjunction with R. Labat's Manuel d'Epigraphie akkadienne (5th ed., Paris: Geuthner, 1976), which gives a more complete list of sign values from all periods of cuneiform writing as well as the sign forms in the major periods. W. von Soden and W. Rollig's Das Akkadische Syllabar (3rd ed., Rome: Pontifical Biblical Institute, 1976) will also be useful in that it presents attestations for the syllabic values in various periods.

I would suggest that the student try to learn three or four signs a day and that he work on them every day for at least a short time so as not to lose the knowledge gained. The student should concentrate on the vocabulary which his teacher recommends and which occurs in the texts he is reading and not pay much attention to that used here. The point throughout this workbook is to learn the signs and not the vocabulary. It has not always been possible to use real words in the examples since, especially at the beginning, the student will not know enough signs. Though this practice may not be scientifically gratifying, there is good precedent for it. (4) In any case, it should be stressed that this manual is intended to teach the practice of recognizing the graphic structure of individual cuneiform signs, not the theory of the graphemic system; hence rare spellings or rare words, as well as sign configurations without lexical meaning, appear justifiable on paedagogical grounds. Note that an asterisk (*) preceding a form given as an example shows that that particular spelling is not actually attested. The number before the first occurrence of the sign indicates its number in Labat's Manuel. (5)

At the end of the workbook one will find an alphabetical index of the values presented here, and there is an index to the signs in the order taught.

I owe a debt of thanks to the students in my beginning Akkadian class at the University of Washington in 1975-1976, and to those in the class of Benjamin Foster at Yale in the same year for their helpful criticisms. Patricia S. Gustafson's help has been important at several stages of the workbook's development, and I am thankful to her. A grant from the Connecticut College Faculty Research and Travel Fund supported the final typing of the manuscript, and the sympathetic support of that institution is deeply appreciated.

I present this workbook in memory of Clair John Snell, who always believed that an intelligent person with a good book could learn anything.

DCS
New London, Connecticut
May 1978

A second printing allowed some corrections to be made in the text. I appreciate especially Daniel Foxvog's review of this work in Language 57:1 (1981), pp. 226-8, many of whose suggestions are incorporated here.

DCS
April 1982

Notes to Introduction

(1) Compare S. Lieberman, The Sumerian Loanwords in Old-Babylonian Akkadian (HSS 22, Missoula: Scholars, 1977), esp. pp. 551-558, for a stimulating application of data on the Japanese writing system to cuneiform problems.

(2) Forthcoming in the series: Cybernetica Mesopotamica: Graphemic Categorization, Undena Publications.

(3) (Leiden: Brill, 1964-). The non-royal corpus was chosen because it is larger than the royal corpus. No attempt was made to compare the two.

(4) See the review of D. H. Roop, An Introduction to the Burmese Writing System (New Haven, 1972) JAOS 95.3 (1975) 536f by J. A. Matisoff. Matisoff observes, "The step-by-step presentation makes it necessary for Roop to use nonsense syllables to illustrate many consonant-vowel combinations. Far from being a defect ..., this trains the student from the outset to view Burmese writing as a logical system that he can use productively. It encourages him to guess at the spelling of words he has heard but not yet seen written down."

(5) The order of the signs goes back apparently to Edwin Norris in 1868; see the note by K. Hecker, ZA 63 (1974) 305 n. 2. --Akkadian words in this workbook are underlined; Sumerian words, usually the logographic reading of the signs, are given all in capitals. A logogram is a sign that stands for an entire word. In Akkadian texts Sumerian words are frequently used to stand for their Akkadian equivalents.

Section One

This workbook is divided into boxes; in the boxes you are to write responses to questions, usually the English pronunciations, termed transliterations, of signs or the signs themselves. To the right of the next box below you will find the correct answer given. Instead of actually filling in the responses one could write responses on paper placed under the box and also covering the correct answer; then one could go through parts of the book several times without having to erase the answers.

The signs will be presented for ease of memory not in the order of our alphabet but in the order of their shapes. This is the order used in Assyriological manuals. The order is from horizontal 𒀸 to 𒌋 to vertical 𒁹 . Each part of the sign is ordered independently so that, for example, all signs that begin with a single wedge come before any that begin with two. Remembering the order of the signs is not important, but it may be useful to remember which signs look like others, how they differ and how they are alike.

Correct answers to questions asked in the larger box on the left above will be given in this column.

1 The first sign is pronounced <u>aš</u>. In Assyriology as in other language studies, <u>š</u> equals English <u>sh</u> as in <u>ship</u>. <u>Aš</u> is written: 𒀸 . Make the wedge first, then draw the line:

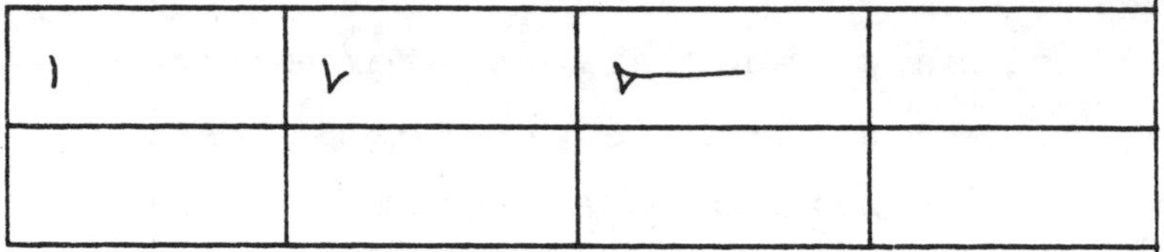

𒀸 is the usual sign in many periods for the syllable ______ .

𒀸 repeated

Carefully copy the sign for <u>aš</u> until you feel confident about remembering it.

<u>aš</u>

aš	aš	aš	aš	aš
aš	aš	aš	aš	aš

What does the symbol <u>š</u> stand for in English writing? ______

𒀸 repeated

<u>sh</u>

The second important sign begins with _____ wedge(s), following the convention that the several signs that begin with one wedge precede those that begin with two.

---

5 It is ba:  .

Copy it carefully, starting with the leftmost wedge and working to the right.

	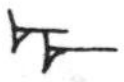	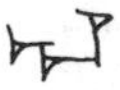	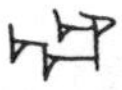	

one

Practice ba until you can remember it.

ba	ba	ba	ba	ba
ba	ba	ba	ba	ba

Transliterate this Akkadian word:

= _____ _____

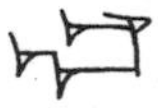

repeated

The sign aš is

The sign ba is

*ba-aš 'to be ashamed' (construct)

6 The sign zu is similar to ba, , but has two verticals instead of one: .
Practice zu:

zu	zu	zu	zu	zu
zu	zu	zu	zu	zu

It is easy to confuse ba, [ ] , and zu, [ ] .

repeated

The group of signs means nothing, but it would be transliterated ________ ________ ________ .

Practice zu and ba until you feel confident you can tell them apart:

aš-ba-zu

zu	ba	zu	ba	zu
ba	zu	ba	zu	ba

---

repeated

13 The next sign is , read DINGIR, the Sumerian word for 'god'. In Akkadian contexts this reading occurs as a determinative before names of gods; in transliteration it appears as a raised d before the gods' names. DINGIR also has a syllabic reading as the syllable <u>an</u>. Only context can determine whether the logographic or syllabic value is meant. Practice it until you think you can remember it: , , .

DINGIR	DINGIR	DINGIR	DINGIR	DINGIR
DINGIR	DINGIR	DINGIR	DINGIR	DINGIR

Transliterate: = ______ ______

= ______ ______

repeated

Put into cuneiform: <u>an-zu-zu</u> '(a spider)'

DINGIR <u>ba</u>
DINGIR <u>aš</u>
(no meanings)

Practice DINGIR.

DINGIR	DINGIR	DINGIR	DINGIR	DINGIR
DINGIR	DINGIR	DINGIR	DINGIR	DINGIR

---

repeated

15 The next sign is ka: . Write it, as usual working from left to right. Note that the top line is not indented as in ba: versus . Try it: , , , .

ka	ka	ka	ka	ka
ka	ka	ka	ka	ka

Transliterate: = ______ ______

= ______ ______

repeated

Remember by its trailing unlike other signs we have seen.
Practice it until you have some confidence with it:

DINGIR-ka
'your god'

ka-aš
'to you'

ka	ka	ka	ka	ka
ka	ka	ka	ka	ka

---

repeated

55 The next sign is la: [cuneiform]. Note that it has three wedges following the initial one. Try it: [cuneiform] , [cuneiform] , [cuneiform] .

la	la	la	la	la
la	la	la	la	la

[cuneiform] repeated

Transliterate: [cuneiform] [cuneiform] = _____ _____

[cuneiform] [cuneiform] [cuneiform] = _____ _____ _____

ka-la 'all'

ba-la-la 'to mix' (accusative)

Put into cuneiform: ba-aš-la 'burnt' (accusative)

[cuneiform]

Put into cuneiform: la-an-ka 'your figure'

[cuneiform]

Practice la until you feel confident about it; draw the wedge first for each line.

la	la	la	la	la
la	la	la	la	la

[cuneiform] repeated

58 The next sign, tu, , begins like la, , but has another above and behind it.

Try tu: , , , .

tu	tu	tu	tu	tu
tu	tu	tu	tu	tu

repeated

Put into cuneiform:

ka-tu 'weak' *zu-tu 'sweat'

Transliterate:

______ ______ ______ ______ ______

and

Practice tu until you gain some confidence with it. The next sign is similar to it, so it would be well to get tu in mind before going on.

tu	tu	tu	tu	tu
tu	tu	tu	tu	tu

tu-zu '(a splendid garment)'
*ka-la-tu 'daughter-in law'

---

repeated

59 The next sign differs from tu, [cuneiform], in that it has another vertical and also in that the top horizontal has a tail. The sign is li, [cuneiform].

Try it: [cuneiform], [cuneiform], [cuneiform], [cuneiform], [cuneiform].

li	li	li	li	li
li	li	li	li	li

Put into cuneiform:

li-la-tu 'night' aš-li 'of a rope'

[cuneiform] repeated

Transliterate:

[cuneiform] [cuneiform] [cuneiform] [cuneiform] [cuneiform] [cuneiform]

_____ _____ _____ _____ _____ _____

[cuneiform] [cuneiform] [cuneiform]

[cuneiform] [cuneiform]

Practice li until you gain some confidence with it. Be sure to keep it distinct in your mind from tu.

li	tu	li	tu	li
li	li	li	li	li

li-ba-aš 'May he come to shame'

li-li-tu 'a demon'

[cuneiform] [cuneiform] repeated

61 The mu sign is . Though simpler than tu and li, it is perhaps harder to make because the trailing wedges are at an angle.

Practice it: , , , .

mu	mu	mu	mu	mu
mu	mu	mu	mu	mu

repeated

Transliterate:

______ ______ ______ ______ ______

mu-tu 'husband'

ka-la-mu 'everything'

Put into cuneiform:

mu-li-la 'sprinkler' (accusative)

li-mu 'eponym'

Practice mu until you feel some confidence with it:

mu	mu	mu	mu	mu
mu	mu	mu	mu	mu

---

repeated

62 The next sign is qa, . Though it resembles ba, , one can remember that it is simpler than ba and has one wedge at an angle. Try it: , , .

qa	qa	qa	qa	qa
qa	qa	qa	qa	qa

Transliterate: = ____ ____

= ____ ____ ____

repeated

Put into cuneiform: ba-qa-mu 'to pluck'

qa-an 'reed of'

qa-aš-tu 'bow'

Also put into cuneiform: qa-tu 'hand'

Practice qa. Be sure to keep it distinct in your mind from ba.

qa	ba	qa	ba	qa
qa	qa	qa	qa	qa

repeated

68 The next sign is ru, [cuneiform]. Draw the horizontal first, then the verticals, then stick in the two diagonal wedges: [cuneiform], [cuneiform], [cuneiform]. Try it:

ru	ru	ru	ru	ru
ru	ru	ru	ru	ru

Transliterate: [cuneiform] [cuneiform] = ______ ______

[cuneiform] [cuneiform] = ______ ______

[cuneiform] repeated

Put into cuneiform:

ba-qa-ru 'to start a law suit'

aš-ru 'place'

ru-tu 'wife'

ru-ba 'noble' (accusative)

Practice ru:

ru	ru	ru	ru	ru
ru	ru	ru	ru	ru

[cuneiform] [cuneiform] [cuneiform]

[cuneiform] [cuneiform]

[cuneiform] repeated

69 The next sign to learn is the sign be, [cuneiform]. Try it: [cuneiform], [cuneiform], [cuneiform].

be	be	be	be	be
be	be	be	be	be

Be should be distinguished from [cuneiform], which is read ______ and which has no tail.

[cuneiform] repeated

Transliterate: [cuneiform] [cuneiform] = ______ ______

[cuneiform] [cuneiform] = ______ ______

aš

Write in cuneiform:

be-li 'my lord'

be-ru '(distance measure of more than 10 kilometers)'

be-la 'lord' (accusative)

ru-be 'nobles'

Practice be and aš to make sure you can keep them apart in your mind.

be	aš	be	aš	be
be	be	be	be	be

[cuneiform] [cuneiform]

[cuneiform] [cuneiform]

[cuneiform] [cuneiform]

repeated

70 The next sign is na, [cuneiform], written [cuneiform], [cuneiform], [cuneiform]. Practice na; one might think of it as be plus part of qa:

na	na	na	na	na
na	na	na	na	na

Transliterate:

[cuneiform] = ____ ____ ____

[cuneiform] = ____ ____ ____

[cuneiform] repeated

Put into cuneiform:

na-ru 'stele'

An-tu '(a goddess)'

na-aš-mu '(a bread or flour)'

ka-na-nu 'to twist'

Practice na until you feel sure of it.

[cuneiform]

na	na	na	na	na
na	na	na	na	na

[cuneiform] repeated

73 The next important sign is ti, , which starts like be: , , , and has a wedge on the other side of its vertical in contrast to na, . Try it:

ti	ti	ti	ti	ti
ti	ti	ti	ti	ti

repeated

Transliterate:

______ ______ ______ ______ ______

Put into cuneiform:

mu-ti 'my husband'			
ti-tu-ru 'bridge'			

qa-ti-ka 'of your hand'

*zu-ti 'of sweat'

Keep ti distinct from na:

ti	na	ti	na	ti
ti	ti	ti	ti	ti

repeated

75 The next sign is <u>nu</u>, which is <u>aš</u> plus a cross stroke running from below to above it: .
Try it:

nu	nu	nu	nu	nu
nu	nu	nu	nu	nu

Transliterate: = _____ _____

= _____ _____ _____

repeated

Put into cuneiform:

<u>ba-nu</u> 'to build'

<u>an-nu</u> 'this'

<u>nu-na</u>
'fish'
(accusative)
<u>nu-ka-tu</u>
'(a plant)'

Practice <u>nu</u> until you feel sure of it.

nu	nu	nu	nu	nu
nu	nu	nu	nu	nu

On the next page is a quiz on all the signs studied so far. Write the signs in the appropriate boxes and turn to the next page for the answers.

repeated

Section One

QUIZ

1. ti	2. aš	3. li
4. mu	5. nu	6. la
7. qa	8. DINGIR	9. be
10. ba	11. na	12. tu
13. ka	14. zu	15. ru

ANSWERS

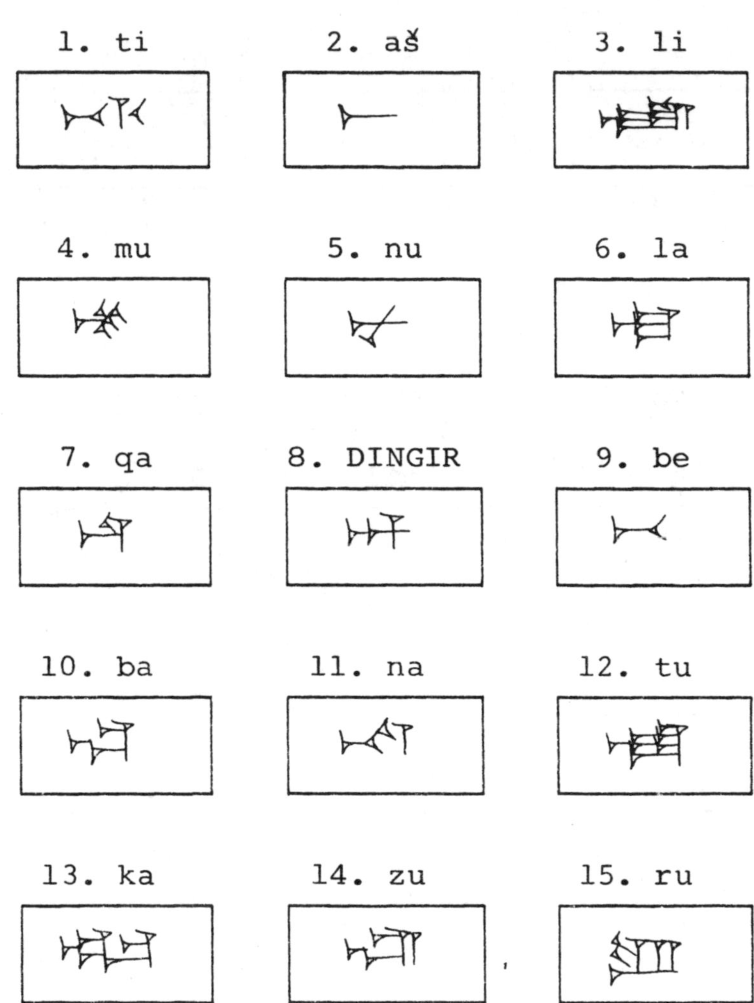

If you forgot one sign, practice it below and then go on. If you forgot more than one, go back to the sections in which the signs were presented and work through them again; then go on to page 19.

Sign _______ :

Section Two

78 The next sign is ḫu, , which starts like be: , , . The symbol ḫ is used to indicate a sound like German ch in Buch or Scottish ch as in loch. Try ḫu:

ḫu ḫu ḫu ḫu ḫu

ḫu ḫu ḫu ḫu ḫu

repeated

Transliterate: = ______ ______

= ______ ______ ______ ______

Put into cuneiform:

na-ḫu 'to rest'

ḫu-li 'of a road'

la-ḫu 'jaw'

*ḫu-la-la-tu '(a stone)'

Practice ḫu:

ḫu ḫu ḫu ḫu ḫu

ḫu ḫu ḫu ḫu ḫu

repeated

79 The next sign is nam, , which begins like ḫu, , but adds four wedges after: . Try it:

nam	nam	nam	nam	nam
nam	nam	nam	nam	nam

repeated

Put into cuneiform:

la-nam 'figure' (accusative)

*nu-nam 'fish' (accusative)

Transliterate:

= ______ ______ ______

= ______ ______

Practice nam until you feel sure of it. Be sure to keep it separate in your mind from ḫu.

nam-ka-ru 'irrigation canal'

nam-ru 'shining'

nam	ḫu	nam	ḫu	nam
nam	nam	nam	nam	nam

repeated

80 The next sign is <u>ik</u>, <u>iq</u>, which begins with <u>ḫu</u> but adds only two wedges: [cuneiform] . Try it:

ik	ik	ik	ik	ik
ik	ik	ik	ik	ik

[cuneiform] repeated

Transliterate:

[cuneiform] = _____ _____

[cuneiform] = _____ _____ _____

Put into cuneiform:

<u>ik-ka-ru</u> 'farmer' <u>ik-mu</u> 'they bound'

<u>ti-iq-nu</u> 'ornament'

<u>ik-ru-ba</u> 'he prayed'

Practice <u>ik</u> and be sure to keep it separate in your mind from <u>nam</u>.

ik	nam	ik	nam	ik
ik	ik	ik	ik	ik

[cuneiform] [cuneiform]

[cuneiform] repeated

84 The sign zi, , begins a new series of shapes. Note especially the arrangement of its last three wedges: , , , .
Try it:

zi	zi	zi	zi	zi
zi	zi	zi	zi	zi

Transliterate: = ______ ______

= ______ ______ ______

repeated

Put into cuneiform:

ka-zi-ru
'(a plant)'

zi-iq-nu
'beard'

zi-mu
'face'

ḫu-zi-ru
'hog'

Practice zi:

zi	zi	zi	zi	zi
zi	zi	zi	zi	zi

---

repeated

85 The next sign, gi, , is easily confused with zi, . Note that the final element in zi is open just as the letter z is open, while that in gi is closed like g. Try gi:

gi	gi	gi	gi	gi
gi	gi	gi	gi	gi

Transliterate: = ______ ______

= ______ ______

repeated

Put into cuneiform:

gi-zi 'of shearing' na-gi-ru 'herald'

gi-na
'regular offering'
(accusative)

mu-gi
'(part of
a title)'
see p. 78

Practice zi and gi.

gi	zi	gi	zi	gi
gi	gi	gi	gi	gi

---

repeated

86 The next sign, ri, re, , resembles hu, , but has one more vertical before the diagonal wedge: , , , . Try it:

ri	ri	ri	ri	ri
ri	ri	ri	ri	ri

Transliterate:

= ______ ______ ______

= ______ ______ ______

repeated

Put into cuneiform:

ri-qa-tu 'empty ones'

ka-ri 'of a quay'

ri-hu-tu 'offspring'

na-ri-ka 'of your stele'

Practice ri. Be sure to keep it distinct in your mind from hu.

ri	hu	ri	hu	ri
ri	ri	ri	ri	ri

---

repeated

94 The next sign is tim, . It begins somewhat like ri, , but has a wedge at the foot of the first vertical and then three slanting wedges forming a triangle.
Try it: , , , .

tim	tim	tim	tim	tim
tim	tim	tim	tim	tim

Transliterate: = ______ ______

= ______ ______

repeated

Put into cuneiform:

tim-mu
'empaling stake'

ba-ru-tim
'of the diviner's craft'

*zu-tim
'of sweat'

qa-tim
'of a hand'

Practice tim until you feel sure of it:

tim	tim	tim	tim	tim
tim	tim	tim	tim	tim

---

repeated

97 The next sign is ak, aq, ag, [cuneiform]. It resembles ka, [cuneiform], though only superficially. Try ak: [cuneiform], [cuneiform], [cuneiform], [cuneiform], [cuneiform].

ak	ak	ak	ak	ak
ak	ak	ak	ak	ak

Transliterate: [cuneiform] [cuneiform] = ______ ______

[cuneiform] [cuneiform] [cuneiform] = ______ ______ ______

[cuneiform] repeated

Put into cuneiform:

ag-gi 'of an angry one' ba-aq-mu 'plucked'

ag-ru 'hired man'

na-ak-ru 'foreign'

Be sure to keep ak and ka distinct in your mind.

ak	ka	ak	ka	ak
ak	ak	ak	ak	ak

[cuneiform] [cuneiform]

[cuneiform] [cuneiform] [cuneiform]

[cuneiform] [cuneiform] repeated

99 The next sign is en, [cuneiform], written [cuneiform], [cuneiform], [cuneiform]. Try it:

en	en	en	en	en
en	en	en	en	en

Transliterate:

[cuneiform] [cuneiform] = ______ ______

[cuneiform] [cuneiform] [cuneiform] = ______ ______ ______

[cuneiform] repeated

Put into cuneiform:

en-zu 'goat'

en-na-na-tim 'a favor' (accusative)

en-tu '(type of priestess)'

be-en-nu '(type of epilepsy)'

Practice en. Be sure to keep it distinct in your mind from ḫu.

en	ḫu	en	ḫu	en
en	en	en	en	en

[cuneiform] [cuneiform]

[cuneiform] [cuneiform]

[cuneiform] [cuneiform]

[cuneiform] [cuneiform] repeated

104 The next sign is sa, , written , , . Be sure to indent the top horizontal, or sa will look like ir, a sign to be learned later. Try sa:

sa	sa	sa	sa	sa
sa	sa	sa	sa	sa

repeated

Transliterate:

= ______ ______ ______

= ______ ______ ______

Put into cuneiform:

*sa-ḫu 'meadow' la-sa-mu 'to run'

sa-ag-ru 'a gold alloy'

*sa-ka-tu 'to be quiet'

Practice sa.

sa	sa	sa	sa	sa
sa	sa	sa	sa	sa

repeated

105 The next sign is IKU, , a logogram for an area measure, with the Akkadian equivalent iků. It is exactly like sa, , except that it has a final vertical. Try it: , , , .

IKU	IKU	IKU	IKU	IKU
IKU	IKU	IKU	IKU	IKU

---

repeated

With IKU the sign aš, , stands for the number one. The aš may be repeated up to five times to express the numbers one through five. Transliterate:

= _____ _____

= _____ _____

---

1 IKU

4 IKU

Put into cuneiform:

3 IKU	

5 IKU	

Practice IKU and sa.

IKU	sa	IKU	sa	IKU
IKU	IKU	IKU	IKU	IKU

---

repeated

111 The next sign is GUR, [cuneiform], a logogram for a volume measure. The Akkadian equivalent is kurru. GUR somewhat resembles IKU, [cuneiform], but it has no interior verticals and two on the end.
Try it: [cuneiform], [cuneiform], [cuneiform], [cuneiform].

GUR	GUR	GUR	GUR	GUR
GUR	GUR	GUR	GUR	GUR

[cuneiform] repeated

With GUR the sign aš, [cuneiform], stands for the number one. The aš may be repeated up to nine times to express the numbers one through nine.
Transliterate: [cuneiform] [cuneiform] = ______ ______

[cuneiform] [cuneiform] = ______ ______

1 GUR
7 GUR

Put into cuneiform:

5 GUR

9 GUR

[cuneiform] [cuneiform]
[cuneiform] [cuneiform]

Practice GUR until you feel sure of it.

GUR	GUR	GUR	GUR	GUR
GUR	GUR	GUR	GUR	GUR

[cuneiform] repeated

112 The next sign is si, , which is exactly like GUR, , except that the top horizontal is longer in si.

Try it: , , , .

si	si	si	si	si
si	si	si	si	si

repeated

Transliterate:

= ____ ____

= ____ ____ ____ ____

Put into cuneiform:

si-ka-tim 'of a nail'

la-si-mu 'messenger'

si-ka-tim 'of a nail'			
la-si-mu 'messenger'			

si-ḫu 'rebellion'

si-si-ik-tu 'hem'

Practice si until you feel some confidence with it. Be sure to keep it distinct in your mind from GUR.

si	GUR	si	GUR	si
si	si	si	si	si

repeated

115 The next sign is SAG, [cuneiform], a logogram for 'head, top', with the Akkadian equivalent rēšu. Its first element is si, [cuneiform], and its second is pa, [cuneiform], a sign to be learned later.
Try it: [cuneiform], [cuneiform], [cuneiform], [cuneiform].

SAG	SAG	SAG	SAG	SAG
SAG	SAG	SAG	SAG	SAG

[cuneiform] repeated

Transliterate:

[cuneiform] = ______ ______ ______

[cuneiform] = ______ ______

SAG mu-tim 'husband's head'

SAG-ka 'your head'

Put into cuneiform:

SAG eq(=ik)-li
'top part of a field'

[cuneiform]

Practice SAG until you feel sure of it.

SAG	SAG	SAG	SAG	SAG
SAG	SAG	SAG	SAG	SAG

[cuneiform] repeated

126 The next sign is šum, , written , , . Try it:

šum	šum	šum	šum	šum
šum	šum	šum	šum	šum

repeated

Transliterate:

= ______ ______ ______

= ______ ______ ______

šum-mu-ḫu 'very luxuriant'

la-aš-šum 'absent'

Put into cuneiform:

en-šum 'weak'

šum-mu 'to consider'

Practice šum until you feel sure of it.

šum	šum	šum	šum	šum
šum	šum	šum	šum	šum

On the next page is a quiz on all the signs studied so far.

repeated

Section Two

QUIZ

1. zi	2. aš	3. SAG	4. ka	5. sa
6. tim	7. IKU	8. ba	9. ri	10. ti
11. nam	12. si	13. ak	14. ḫu	15. DINGIR
16. ik	17. li	18. nu	19. šum	20. mu
21. gi	22. tu	23. en	24. na	25. qa
26. GUR	27. ru	28. zu	29. la	30. be

ANSWERS

1.	2.	3.	4.	5.
6.	7.	8.	9.	10.
11.	12.	13.	14.	15.
16.	17.	18.	19.	20.
21.	22.	23.	24.	25.
26.	27.	28.	29.	30.

If you forgot one sign, practice it here and then go on to Section Three. If you forgot more than one, go back to the places where they were first presented and work through the parts dealing with them; then go on to Section Three.

Sign ________ :

Section Three

128 The next sign is ab, ap, . It begins exactly like šum, , but instead of a diagonal it has a vertical at the end.
Try it: , , .

ab	ab	ab	ab	ab
ab	ab	ab	ab	ab

repeated

Put into cuneiform:

ba-ab-tu 'city quarter' ap-tu 'window'

Transliterate:

= ____ ____

= ____ ____ ____ ____

ab-nu 'stone'
*qa-ab-li-tu 'middle'

Practice ab and be sure to keep it distinct in your mind from šum.

ab	šum	ab	šum	ab
ab	ab	ab	ab	ab

repeated

130 The next sign, uk, uq, ug, [cuneiform], begins like ab but has two elements inscribed. The last element in uk is [cuneiform], the sign UTU, to be learned later. Its presence may be a memory aid to remind scribes that uk, like UTU, begins with the sound u. Try uk: [cuneiform], [cuneiform], [cuneiform], [cuneiform].

uk	uk	uk	uk	uk
uk	uk	uk	uk	uk

[cuneiform] repeated

Transliterate:

[cuneiform] [cuneiform] = _____ _____

[cuneiform] [cuneiform] [cuneiform] = _____ _____ _____

uk-la 'dark' (accusative)

ru-uq-tu 'far' (feminine)

Put into cuneiform:

zu-uk-ti 'of the chin'

tu-uk-ka-an-nu 'bag'

[cuneiform]

Practice uk until you feel sure of it.

uk	uk	uk	uk	uk
uk	uk	uk	uk	uk

[cuneiform] repeated

131 The sign as, az, aṣ, [cuneiform], is exactly like uk except for the last interior element. This element is the sign ṣa, [cuneiform], which will be learned later; it may have been put in as to remind scribes that the sounds which as represented also included a sound ṣ. (Ṣ is the transliteration for a sybillant conventionally pronounced as if it were English ts.)

Try as: [cuneiform], [cuneiform], [cuneiform].

as	as	as	as	as
as	as	as	as	as

Transliterate:

[cuneiform] = ____ ____

[cuneiform] = ____ ____ ____ ____

[cuneiform] repeated

---

as-la 'young sheep' (accusative)

na-aṣ-ba-ru '(part of a door)'

Put into cuneiform:

as-mu 'fitting'

ka-as-ka-zu '(part of a sheep's breast-bone)'

Practice as and uk until you are sure of them.

as	uk	as	uk	as
as	as	as	as	as

---

repeated

134 The next sign, um, , again begins more or less like ab, , but has three final verticals instead of one: , , , . Try um.

um	um	um	um	um
um	um	um	um	um

Transliterate:

= _____ _____ _____

= _____ _____ _____ _____

repeated

Put into cuneiform:

ba-nu-um 'well-formed'			
qa-tu-um 'hand'			

um-mu-um 'mother'

na-ak-ru-um 'foreign'

Practice um, as, and uk.

um	as	uk	um	as
uk	**um**	**as**	**uk**	**um**
as	**uk**	**um**	**as**	**uk**

repeated

139 The next sign is ta, [cuneiform]. Like um, [cuneiform], it ends in three verticals but begins differently: [cuneiform], [cuneiform], [cuneiform], [cuneiform], [cuneiform]. Try it:

ta	ta	ta	ta	ta
ta	ta	ta	ta	ta

[cuneiform] repeated

Transliterate:

[cuneiform] = ____ ____ ____

[cuneiform] = ____ ____ ____ ____ ____

ta-aš-ba 'you became satisfied'

ta-ba-aš-ta-nu 'excrement'

Put into cuneiform:

ka-ta-mu 'to cover'

ta-ab-ri-tim 'of a report of arrival'

[cuneiform]

Practice ta and um until you feel sure you can tell them apart.

ta	um	ta	um	ta
ta	ta	ta	ta	ta

[cuneiform] repeated

142 The next sign, i, [cuneiform], has no verticals: [cuneiform], [cuneiform]. Try it:

i	i	i	i	i
i	i	i	i	i

Transliterate:

[cuneiform] = ____ ____ ____ ____

[cuneiform] = ____ ____ ____

[cuneiform] repeated

Put into cuneiform:

i-ta-mu 'he addressed'   i-li 'my god'

i-ba-qa-ru 'they start a law suit'

ri-i-ti 'of a pasture'

Practice i until you feel sure of it.

i	i	i	i	i
i	i	i	i	i

[cuneiform]

[cuneiform]

[cuneiform]

repeated

142a The next sign is ia, , which is simply a combination of i, , and a, , a sign to be learned later.

Try it: , , , .

ia	ia	ia	ia	ia
ia	ia	ia	ia	ia

repeated

Transliterate:

= ______ ______ ______

= ______ ______ ______

be-li-ia 'of my lord'

qa-ti-ia 'of my hand'

Put into cuneiform:

ia-nu 'it is not'   ia-mu-tu 'each'

Practice ia until you feel sure of it. Keep it distinct in your mind from i.

ia	i	ia	i	ia
ia	ia	ia	ia	ia

---

repeated

144 The next sign is DUMU, [cuneiform], a logogram meaning 'son', with the Akkadian translation māru. It is exactly like i, [cuneiform], except that it has a vertical wedge inserted at the rear.
Try it: [cuneiform], [cuneiform], [cuneiform].

DUMU	DUMU	DUMU	DUMU	DUMU
DUMU	DUMU	DUMU	DUMU	DUMU

Transliterate:

[cuneiform] = ____ ____ ____

[cuneiform] = ____ ____ ____ ____

[cuneiform] repeated

Put into cuneiform:

DUMU ru-be 'nobleman'

i-na DUMU-ka 'in your son'

*DUMU mu-ti 'husband's son'

DUMU ba-nu-tu 'status of a free person'

Practice DUMU and be sure to keep it distinct in your mind from i:

DUMU	i	DUMU	i	DUMU
DUMU	DUMU	DUMU	DUMU	DUMU

[cuneiform]

[cuneiform] repeated

145 At, ad, , begins like i, , but has a final vertical: , , .
Try it:

at	at	at	at	at
at	at	at	at	at

Transliterate:

= _____ _____ _____

repeated

= _____ _____

Put into cuneiform:

at-tu-nu 'you' (plural)

qa-at 'hand of'

ba-at-ti 'of surroundings'

aṣ-ba-at 'I got'

Practice at to distinguish it from ab.

at	ab	at	ab	at
at	at	at	at	at

repeated

147 The next sign is ṣi, [cuneiform], which is at, [cuneiform], plus another vertical. Try it:

ṣi	ṣi	ṣi	ṣi	ṣi
ṣi	ṣi	ṣi	ṣi	ṣi

Transliterate:

[cuneiform] [cuneiform] = _____ _____

[cuneiform] [cuneiform] [cuneiform] = _____ _____ _____

[cuneiform] repeated

Put into cuneiform:

ṣi-ru 'extraordinary' | ṣi-nu 'evil'

tu-ṣi 'you went out'

ṣi-i-tu 'going out'

Practice ṣi to keep it distinct in your mind from at.

ṣi	at	ṣi	at	ṣi
ṣi	ṣi	ṣi	ṣi	ṣi

[cuneiform] [cuneiform]

[cuneiform] [cuneiform]

[cuneiform] [cuneiform] repeated

148 The next sign is in, , written , , , . Try it:

in	in	in	in	in
in	in	in	in	in

Transliterate: = ______ ______ ; repeated

= ______ ______

Put into cuneiform: in-ba 'fruit' (accusative); in-ḫu 'suffering'

gi-in-nu 'mark'

i-in 'eye of'

Practice in until you are sure of it.

in	in	in	in	in
in	in	in	in	in

repeated

152 The next sign is šar, , which begins with two horizontals and somewhat resembles ka, , at the end. Try it: , , , .

šar	šar	šar	šar	šar
šar	šar	šar	šar	šar

repeated

Transliterate:

= ____ ____ ____

= ____ ____ ____

Put into cuneiform:

šar-ri-ru 'stooping'

šar-ti 'of hair'

šar-ru-tu 'kingship'

i-šar-tu 'righteousness'

Practice šar until you feel sure of it. Keep it distinct in your mind from ka.

šar	ka	šar	ka	šar
šar	šar	šar	šar	šar

---

repeated

170 The next sign is am, , written , , . Try it:

am	am	am	am	am
am	am	am	am	am

Transliterate:

= ____ ____

= ____ ____ ____

repeated

Put into cuneiform:

*ta-am-tu 'sea'

am-na-am 'I counted out'

am-si 'I washed'

aš-la-am 'rope' (accusative)

Practice am.

am	am	am	am	am
am	am	am	am	am

repeated

172 The next sign is bí, . The acute accent on the bí shows that this sign is the second in theoretical frequency in signs that are read bi. A grave accent, ` , would show a sign is third in frequency. After that subscribed numbers are used to distinguish signs in transliteration, like bi_5. Bí is sometimes read ne. Bí is composed of am, , plus GIŠ, , a sign to be learned later.

Try bí: , , , .

bí	bí	bí	bí	bí
bí	bí	bí	bí	bí

repeated

Transliterate:

= ____ ____ ____

= ____ ____ ____ ____

*ne-zu-tim 'remote' (feminine plural)

na-bi-ḫu-um 'an ornament'

Put into cuneiform:

mu-šar-bí 'increaser of ...' *qa-bí 'is said'

Practice bí and am.

bí	am	bí	am	bí
bí	bí	bí	bí	bí

repeated

191 The next sign is kum, qum, qu, [cuneiform], which is one aš, [cuneiform], and three be's, [cuneiform].
Try it: [cuneiform], [cuneiform], [cuneiform].

kum	kum	kum	kum	kum
kum	kum	kum	kum	kum

[cuneiform] repeated

Transliterate:

[cuneiform] [cuneiform] = ____ ____

[cuneiform] [cuneiform] [cuneiform] = ____ ____ ____

kum-mu 'private room'

ka-ak-kum 'weapon'

Put into cuneiform:

sa-na-qum 'to check' šar-kum 'puss'

[cuneiform] [cuneiform]

[cuneiform]

[cuneiform] [cuneiform]

Practice kum until you are sure of it.

kum	kum	kum	kum	kum
kum	kum	kum	kum	kum

[cuneiform] repeated

On the next page is a quiz over all the signs studied so far.

Section Three

QUIZ

1. ak	2. tu	3. kum	4. ia	5. be
6. li	7. SAG	8. qa	9. zu	10. ru
11. sa	12. in	13. zi	14. tim	15. ik
16. šum	17. ta	18. DUMU	19. šar	20. uk
21. gi	22. DINGIR	23. bí	24. ri	25. ḫu
26. la	27. si	28. GUR	29. i	30. at
31. am	32. ti	33. ab	34. nu	35. as
36. na	37. ka	38. um	39. ṣi	40. mu
41. nam	42. ba	43. aš	44. en	45. IKU

ANSWERS

1.	2.	3.	4.	5.
6.	7.	8.	9.	10.
11.	12.	13.	14.	15.
16.	17.	18.	19.	20.
21.	22.	23.	24.	25.
26.	27.	28.	29.	30.
31.	32.	33.	34.	35.
36.	37.	38.	39.	40.
41.	42.	43.	44.	45.

If you forgot a sign, practice it here and then go on to Section Four. If you forgot more than one, go back to the parts where they were presented and do the exercises for those signs. Then go on to Section Four.

Sign ________ :

Section Four

205 The next sign is il, [cuneiform] , made [cuneiform] , [cuneiform] , [cuneiform] , [cuneiform] . Try it:

il	il	il	il	il
il	il	il	il	il

Transliterate:

[cuneiform] = ____ ____ ____

[cuneiform] = ____ ____ ____

[cuneiform] repeated

Put into cuneiform:

il-li 'of a playmate'

il-ka
'service performed'
(accusative)

il-la-ak 'he goes'

li-il-qa 'let him take'

Remember that il has two verticals as well as two diagonals. Practice il:

il	il	il	il	il
il	il	il	il	il

[cuneiform] [cuneiform]

[cuneiform] [cuneiform]

[cuneiform] repeated

206 Du, , is il, , without the two diagonals and with only one vertical: , , , . Try it:

du	du	du	du	du
du	du	du	du	du

Transliterate: = ___ ___

= ___ ___

repeated

Put into cuneiform:

du-ru 'wall'

qa-du 'with'

du-um 'it is very dark'

mu-du 'expert'

Practice du and il until you feel sure of them.

du	il	du	il	du
du	du	du	du	du

---

repeated

207 The next sign is tum, . It begins somewhat like du, , but ends in four horizontals. Try it: , , , .

tum	tum	tum	tum	tum
tum	tum	tum	tum	tum

Transliterate:

= ____ ____

= ____ ____ ____ ____

repeated

Put into cuneiform:

šar-tum 'hair'

nu-ka-sa-tum 'meat trimmings'

tum-ru 'glowing coals'

du-mu-uq-tum 'good luck'

Practice tum until you feel sure of it.

tum	tum	tum	tum	tum
tum	tum	tum	tum	tum

---

repeated

211 The next sign is uš, : , , . Try it:

uš	uš	uš	uš	uš
uš	uš	uš	uš	uš

repeated

Transliterate:

= ____ ____ ____

= ____ ____ ____ ____

ru-uš-ti 'of fine oil'

mu-uš-ta-li 'of a judicious person'

Put into cuneiform:

uš-ba 'he sat' tu-uš-ru '(a plant)'

Practice uš until you feel sure of it.

uš	uš	uš	uš	uš
uš	uš	uš	uš	uš

repeated

212 The next sign, <u>iš</u>, 𒅖, resembles <u>uš</u>, 𒍑, but lacks the two interior verticals and has two at the end: 𒁹, 𒁹, 𒅖.
Try it:

iš	iš	iš	iš	iš
iš	iš	iš	iš	iš

𒅖 repeated

Transliterate:

𒅖 𒌅 = _____ _____

𒊑 𒅖 𒈬 = _____ _____ _____

<u>iš-tu</u> 'from'

<u>li-iš-mu</u> 'let them hear'

Put into cuneiform:

<u>ri-iš-tum</u> 'jubilation'

<u>iš-ka-ru</u> 'assigned work'

𒊑 𒅖 𒌈

𒅖 𒋾 𒅗

Practice <u>iš</u> and <u>uš</u> until you feel sure you can tell them apart.

iš	uš	iš	uš	iš
iš	iš	iš	iš	iš

𒅖 𒍑 repeated

214 The next sign bi, , is composed of two be's, . Try it: , .

bi	bi	bi	bi	bi
bi	bi	bi	bi	bi

Transliterate:

= ____ ____

= ____ ____ ____

repeated

Put into cuneiform:

bi-ri-tim 'of an alley'

ti-bi 'of an attack'

bi-tu 'house'

in-bi-ka 'of your fruit'

Bi is a simple sign; the only problem with it is to keep it distinct in your mind from be. Practice both.

bi	be	bi	be	bi
bi	bi	bi	bi	bi

repeated

231 The next sign is ni, [cuneiform], made [cuneiform], [cuneiform], [cuneiform]. Try it:

ni	ni	ni	ni	ni
ni	ni	ni	ni	ni

Transliterate:

[cuneiform] = ____ ____ ____

[cuneiform] = ____ ____ ____ ____

[cuneiform] repeated

Put into cuneiform:

ni-du-tu 'unworked land'			
an-ni-um 'this'			

an-ni-iš 'here'

ni-sa-an-nu '(a month-name)'

Practice ni until you feel sure of it.

ni	ni	ni	ni	ni
ni	ni	ni	ni	ni

[cuneiform]

[cuneiform]

[cuneiform] repeated

232 The next sign ir, er, 𒅕 , is exactly like ni, 𒉌 , except that it has one more vertical: 𒁹 , 𒁹 , 𒁹 , 𒅕 . Try it:

ir	ir	ir	ir	ir
ir	ir	ir	ir	ir

Transliterate:

𒁍 𒅕 𒄣 = _____ _____ _____

𒅕 𒉌 𒋾 𒅎 = _____ _____ _____ _____

𒅕 repeated

Put into cuneiform:

bi-ir-qu 'lightning'			
gi-ir-ru 'road'			

i-ir-ti 'of a breast'

ir-ni-ta-ka 'your victory' (accusative)

Practice ir. Remember only one vertical keeps it from being ni.

ir	ni	ir	ni	ir
ir	ir	ir	ir	ir

𒄿 𒅕 𒋾

𒅕 𒉌 𒋫 𒅗

𒅕 𒉌 repeated

295 The next sign is pa, . Beginning like ni, , it has a single vertical that cuts both lines: , , . Try it:

pa	pa	pa	pa	pa
pa	pa	pa	pa	pa

---

repeated

Put into cuneiform:

pa-aš-tu 'dagger'

pa-ag-ru 'body'

Transliterate:

= ______ ______

= ______ ______ ______ ______ ______

---

pa-du 'to shut in'

i-na pa-ni-ka 'before you'

Practice pa until you feel sure you know it.

pa	pa	pa	pa	pa
pa	pa	pa	pa	pa

---

repeated

296 The next sign is GIŠ, [cuneiform], a logogram for 'wood' with the Akkadian equivalent iṣu. It is also used as a determinative before names of wooden objects. Further, it has the value is (iz, iṣ) as a syllabic value. It is exactly like pa, [cuneiform], except that its horizontals do not cut the vertical. Try it: [cuneiform], [cuneiform].

GIŠ	GIŠ	GIŠ	GIŠ	GIŠ
GIŠ	GIŠ	GIŠ	GIŠ	GIŠ

[cuneiform] repeated

Transliterate: [cuneiform] [cuneiform] = _____ _____

[cuneiform] [cuneiform] [cuneiform] = _____ _____ _____

bi-is 'thereafter'

GIŠ.AB.BA =kušabku '(a thorn tree)'

Put into cuneiform:

ni-is-sa-tu 'lament'

GIŠ.GI(=apu) 'reed thicket'

[cuneiform] [cuneiform] [cuneiform] [cuneiform]

[cuneiform] [cuneiform]

Practice GIŠ until you feel sure of it. Keep it distinct in your mind from pa.

GIŠ	pa	GIŠ	pa	GIŠ
GIŠ	GIŠ	GIŠ	GIŠ	GIŠ

[cuneiform] [cuneiform] repeated

297 The next sign is GU_4, [cuneiform], a logogram for 'ox' with the Akkadian equivalent <u>alpu</u>. It is GIŠ with two diagonals following. Try it: [cuneiform], [cuneiform], [cuneiform].

GU_4	GU_4	GU_4	GU_4	GU_4
GU_4	GU_4	GU_4	GU_4	GU_4

Transliterate: [cuneiform] [cuneiform] = _____ _____

[cuneiform] [cuneiform] = _____ _____

[cuneiform] repeated

Put into cuneiform:

d(=DINGIR)GU_4.AN(=DINGIR).NA

(logogram for the god Amurru)

GU_4.GIŠ=<u>alap nīri</u> 'yoke ox'

GU_4.AM=<u>rīmu</u> 'wild steer'

Practice GU_4 until you feel sure of it. Be sure to keep it distinct in your mind from GIŠ.

GU_4	GIŠ	GU_4	GIŠ	GU_4
GU_4	GU_4	GU_4	GU_4	GU_4

[cuneiform] [cuneiform] [cuneiform] [cuneiform]

[cuneiform] [cuneiform] repeated

298 The next sign, al, [cuneiform], begins with GIŠ but has an additional [cuneiform]. It is written [cuneiform], [cuneiform], [cuneiform], [cuneiform], [cuneiform].

Try it:

al	al	al	al	al
al	al	al	al	al

Transliterate:

[cuneiform] = ____ ____ ____ ____

[cuneiform] = ____ ____ ____ ____

[cuneiform] repeated

Put into cuneiform:

na-al-ba-nu 'brick mold'

al-li 'of a hoe'

la-al-la-ru 'lamentation priest'

ta-al-la-ak 'you go'

Practice al until you feel sure of it.

al	al	al	al	al
al	al	al	al	al

[cuneiform]

[cuneiform] repeated

306 The next sign is up, ub, [cuneiform], which begins like GIŠ, [cuneiform], but has diagonal wedges attached: [cuneiform], [cuneiform], [cuneiform], [cuneiform], [cuneiform]. Try it:

up	up	up	up	up
up	up	up	up	up

[cuneiform] repeated

Transliterate:

[cuneiform] = _____ _____ _____

[cuneiform] = _____ _____ _____

i-ru-ub 'he entered'

nu-up-tu 'special gift'

Put into cuneiform:

ḫu-ub-tim 'of robbery'

ḫu-ub-ta-tu 'a type of loan'

[cuneiform]

Practice up until you feel sure of it.

up	up	up	up	up
up	up	up	up	up

[cuneiform] repeated

308 The next sign is e, . It too starts like GIŠ, , but has another vertical made up of two smaller verticals: , , . Try it:

e	e	e	e	e
e	e	e	e	e

Transliterate: = _____ _____

= _____ _____ _____

repeated

Put into cuneiform:

na-re-e 'of a monument'

e-gi-tu 'negligence'

e-mu 'father-in-law'

e-li-iš 'on top'

Practice e until you are sure you can recognize it.

e	e	e	e	e
e	e	e	e	e

---

repeated

318 The next sign is ú, . The acute accent on the u indicates that this sign is the second in theoretical frequency of signs that are read u. Ú begins with GIŠ. Try ú: , , .

ú	ú	ú	ú	ú
ú	ú	ú	ú	ú

Transliterate:

= _____ _____ _____ _____ _____

= _____ _____ _____

repeated

Put into cuneiform:

ú-na-ak-ka-ru 'they change'

ba-nu-ú 'excellent'

ú-ub-la 'he brought me'			
ú-nu-tu 'utensil'			

Practice ú until you feel sure of it.

ú	ú	ú	ú	ú
ú	ú	ú	ú	ú

On the next page is a quiz on all the signs studied so far.

repeated

Section Four

QUIZ

1. be	2. ba	3. ab	4. ru	5. nam	6. GU_4
7. al	8. nu	9. uk	10. IKU	11. kum	12. bi
13. GIŠ	14. zu	15. GUR	16. sa	17. šar	18. ṣi
19. tum	20. tu	21. zi	22. pa	23. li	24. aš
25. il	26. ni	27. ri	28. as	29. ka	30. ú
31. ir	32. um	33. tim	34. mu	35. en	36. up
37. in	38. la	39. iš	40. ti	41. SAG	42. am
43. ak	44. DUMU	45. uš	46. na	47. i	48. ḫu
49. qa	50. du	51. e	52. bí	53. šum	54. gi
55. ia	56. ta	57. ik	58. si	59. at	60. DINGIR

ANSWERS

1.	2.	3.	4.	5.	6.
7.	8.	9.	10.	11.	12.
13.	14.	15.	16.	17.	18.
19.	20.	21.	22.	23.	24.
25.	26.	27.	28.	29.	30.
31.	32.	33.	34.	35.	36.
37.	38.	39.	40.	41.	42.
43.	44.	45.	46.	47.	48.
49.	50.	51.	52.	53.	54.
55.	56.	57.	58.	59.	60.

If you missed a sign, practice it here. If you missed more than one, go back to the part where each sign was first presented and work through it again. Then go on to Section Five.

Sign ________ :

Section Five

319 The next sign is qá, ga, [cuneiform], which is like ú, [cuneiform], except for its final diagonals. Try it: [cuneiform], [cuneiform], [cuneiform].

qá	qá	qá	qá	qá
qá	qá	qá	qá	qá

Transliterate: [cuneiform] = ____ ____ ____

[cuneiform] = ____ ____ ____

[cuneiform] repeated

Put into cuneiform:

la-ga-ru 'type of priest'

ta-qá-an-ni 'you will retain'

ga-la-tu 'to shake with fear'

qá-qá-ri 'of earth'

Practice qá. Be sure to keep it distinct from ú.

qá	ú	qá	ú	qá
qá	qá	qá	qá	qá

[cuneiform] [cuneiform] repeated

324 The next sign is É, [cuneiform], a logogram for 'house' with the Akkadian translation <u>bītu</u>. It is very much like <u>ú</u>, [cuneiform], but it has four verticals and no trailing horizontals. Try it: [cuneiform], [cuneiform], [cuneiform].

É	É	É	É	É
É	É	É	É	É

[cuneiform] repeated

Transliterate: [cuneiform] [cuneiform] = ____ ____

[cuneiform] [cuneiform] = ____ ____

DUMU.É= <u>mār bīti</u> 'administrator of a household'

É.GU_4= <u>bīt alpi</u> 'cattle shed'

Put into cuneiform:

É <u>du-ri</u> 'fortress'

É <u>gi-iz-zi</u> 'shearing shed'

[cuneiform] [cuneiform]

[cuneiform] [cuneiform]

[cuneiform]

Practice É until you feel sure of it. Keep it distinct in your mind from <u>ú</u>.

É	É	É	É	É
É	ú	É	ú	É

[cuneiform] [cuneiform] repeated

328 The next sign is <u>ra</u>, , written , , , . Try it:

ra	ra	ra	ra	ra
ra	ra	ra	ra	ra

Transliterate: = _____ _____ _____

= _____ _____ _____

repeated

Put into cuneiform:

<u>ra-pa-aš-tum</u> 'wide'

<u>na-ra-am-tu</u> 'beloved'

<u>ra-ga-mu</u> 'to yell'

<u>ba-ra-mu</u> 'to be or become multicolored'

Practice <u>ra</u> until you feel sure of it.

ra	ra	ra	ra	ra
ra	ra	ra	ra	ra

---

repeated

330 The next sign is LÚ, , a logogram for 'man', translated by Akkadian amīlu. It is also used as a determinative before names of professions. LÚ begins like ra, , but ends with three horizontals above three verticals.

Try it: , , .

LÚ	LÚ	LÚ	LÚ	LÚ
LÚ	LÚ	LÚ	LÚ	LÚ

Transliterate:

= ____ ____ ____ ____

= ____ ____

(answer: repeated)

Put into cuneiform:

LÚ ta-am-ka-ru 'merchant'

LÚ e-ṣi-ra 'relief carver' (accusative)

(answers: LÚ la-si-mu 'messenger'; SAG.LÚ = rēš amīli 'a man's head')

Practice LÚ and in, which is similar to it.

LÚ	in	LÚ	in	LÚ
LÚ	LÚ	LÚ	LÚ	LÚ

(answer: repeated)

334 The next sign is it, iṭ, id, , which resembles am, , with an additional "broken" horizontal and vertical: , , , . Try it:

it	it	it	it	it
it	it	it	it	it

Transliterate:

= ____ ____

= ____ ____ ____ ____

repeated

Put into cuneiform:

bi-it-ru-ú 'superb'

zi-it-tu 'share'

it-bi 'he got up'

id-ra-nu-um 'potash'

Practice it until you feel sure of it.

it	it	it	it	it
it	it	it	it	it

repeated

335 Da, , is very like it, but da has two verticals: , , , , .
Try it:

da	da	da	da	da
da	da	da	da	da

Transliterate:

= _____ _____ _____

= _____ _____ _____

repeated

Put into cuneiform:

da-an-nu 'strong'			
da-al-tu 'door'			

ka-da-du 'to rub'
da-ri-iš 'forever'

Practice da and be sure to keep it distinct in your mind from it.

da	it	da	it	da
da	da	da	da	da

repeated

342 The next sign is ma, [cuneiform], written: [cuneiform], [cuneiform], [cuneiform]. Try it:

ma	ma	ma	ma	ma
ma	ma	ma	ma	ma

[cuneiform] repeated

Put into cuneiform:

ma-al-ka-am 'advice' (accusative)

ú-ma-al-li 'he filled'

[cuneiform]

Transliterate:

[cuneiform] = ____ ____ ____

[cuneiform] = ____ ____ ____

[cuneiform]

Practice ma until you feel sure of it.

ma-da-du 'to measure'

ma-ga-ru 'to approve'

ma	ma	ma	ma	ma
ma	ma	ma	ma	ma

[cuneiform] repeated

343 The next sign is GAL, gal, , logogram for 'great', translated by Akkadian rabû. It is ma, , with a trailing horizontal. Try it: , , .

GAL	GAL	GAL	GAL	GAL
GAL	GAL	GAL	GAL	GAL

repeated

Transliterate:

= ___ ___ ___

= ___ ___ ___ ___

Put into cuneiform:

DINGIR.GAL=ilu rabû 'great god'

GAL mu-qi 'general'

šar-ru GAL 'great king'

*GAL bi-tu-tu 'office of the chief of the house'

Practice GAL until you feel sure of it. Keep it distinct in your mind from ma.

GAL	ma	GAL	ma	GAL
GAL	GAL	GAL	GAL	GAL

repeated

353 The next sign is <u>ša</u>, 𒊭 , similar to <u>da</u>, 𒁕 , but with four horizontals: , , , . Try it:

ša	ša	ša	ša	ša
ša	ša	ša	ša	ša

𒊭 repeated

Transliterate: 𒊭 𒁕 = ____ ____

𒊭 𒈠 = ____ ____

<u>ša-du</u> 'mountain'

<u>ša-mu</u> 'to buy'

Put into cuneiform:

<u>ša-la-mu</u> 'to be whole'			
<u>ga-ša-ru</u> 'to be strong'			

Practice <u>ša</u> and <u>da</u>.

𒊭 𒆷 𒈬 𒂵 𒊭 𒊒

ša	da	ša	da	ša
ša	ša	ša	ša	ša

𒊭 𒁕 repeated

354 The next sign is <u>šu</u>, [cuneiform] : [cuneiform] , [cuneiform] , [cuneiform] . Unlike <u>ša</u>, <u>šu</u>'s bottom horizontal is longer than the others. Try it:

šu	šu	šu	šu	šu
šu	šu	šu	šu	šu

Transliterate: [cuneiform] = ____ ____ ____

[cuneiform] = ____ ____ ____

[cuneiform] repeated

Put into cuneiform:

<u>šu-bi-la</u> 'send to me'

<u>re-šu</u> 'head'

<u>šu-ub-nu</u> 'to cause to build'

<u>e-li-šu</u> 'on him'

Practice <u>šu</u>.

šu	šu	šu	šu	šu
šu	šu	šu	šu	šu

[cuneiform]

[cuneiform]

[cuneiform] repeated

367 The next sign is <u>še</u>, [cuneiform] , which is the second element in the sign <u>mu</u>, [cuneiform] . It is written [cuneiform] , [cuneiform] , [cuneiform] . Try it:

še	še	še	še	še
še	še	še	še	še

Answer: [cuneiform] repeated

Transliterate:

[cuneiform] [cuneiform] = ____ ____

[cuneiform] [cuneiform] [cuneiform] [cuneiform] = ____ ____ ____ ____

<u>še-ú</u> 'barley'; <u>mu-še-še-er</u> 'one who puts in order'

Put into cuneiform:

<u>še-mu</u> 'to hear'

<u>ni-še</u> 'lions'

[cuneiform] [cuneiform] [cuneiform] [cuneiform]

Practice <u>še</u> until you feel sure of it.

še	še	še	še	še
še	še	še	še	še

Answer: [cuneiform] repeated

371 The next sign is <u>pu</u>, <u>bu</u>, , which is <u>še</u> plus <u>aš</u>, + . Try it:

pu	pu	pu	pu	pu
pu	pu	pu	pu	pu

---

repeated

Transliterate: = _____ _____

= _____ _____ _____

---

na-bu 'to call'

pu-ri-du 'leg'

Put into cuneiform:

pu-ḫu 'replacement' bu-uq-li 'of malt'

pu	ḫu

bu	uq	li

Practice <u>pu</u> to keep it distinct in your mind from <u>mu</u>.

pu	mu	pu	mu	pu
pu	pu	pu	pu	pu

---

repeated

376 The next sign is te, [cuneiform], which is še, [cuneiform], plus a vertical. Try it: .

te	te	te	te	te
te	te	te	te	te

Transliterate: [cuneiform] = ____ ____

[cuneiform] = ____ ____ ____

[cuneiform] repeated

Put into cuneiform:

te-ru-ub 'you entered'

te-er-tum 'omen'

te-bu 'to rise up'

te-nu-ú 'pendant'

Practice te and pu.

te	pu	te	pu	te
te	te	te	te	te

[cuneiform]

[cuneiform]

[cuneiform] repeated

381 The next sign, , has several values. The following logographic values are most common: dUTU = Šamaš 'the sun god', BABBAR = peṣû 'white, shining', and U_4 = ūmu 'day'. It also has the syllabic values tam and ut, ud. We will refer to it as the UTU sign, but only the context can show you which reading to use. UTU is the last element inscribed in the sign uk, . Try it:

UTU	UTU	UTU	UTU	UTU
UTU	UTU	UTU	UTU	UTU

Transliterate:

= _____ _____ _____ _____ _____ _____ _____

= _____ _____ _____

repeated

---

^{d}UTU-mu-ba-al-li-iṭ 'Šamaš-makes live' (a personal name)

tam-gi-ti 'of a joyous song'

Put into cuneiform:

<u>li-mu-ut-tim</u> 'of wickedness'

<u>šar-ra-tam</u> 'queen' (accusative)

Practice UTU until you feel sure of it. Recognizing its various values will come with practice.

UTU	UTU	UTU	UTU	UTU
UTU	UTU	UTU	UTU	UTU

---

repeated

383 The next sign is wa, , also read wi, wu, or pi. It consists of UTU, , plus aš, . Try it:

wa	wa	wa	wa	wa
wa	wa	wa	wa	wa

Transliterate: = ___ ___ ___

= ___ ___ ___

repeated

Put into cuneiform:

wu-uš-šu-ru 'to liberate'

pi-it-qa 'fashioning'

wa-la-du 'to give birth'

wa-qa-ru 'to be costly'

As you see, it is context only that determines the reading of wa. Practice wa until you are sure of it, and keep it distinct in your mind from UTU.

wa	UTU	wa	UTU	wa
wa	wa	wa	wa	wa

On the next pages is a quiz on all the signs studied so far.

repeated

Section Five

QUIZ

1. šar	2. i	3. gi	4. mu	5. bí
6. aš	7. tum	8. pa	9. ḫu	10. si
11. la	12. ma	13. ir	14. zu	15. am
16. ru	17. il	18. DUMU	19. uk	20. UTU
21. ab	22. uš	23. zi	24. ba	25. in
26. tu	27. bi	28. da	29. SAG	30. ka
31. du	32. kum	33. ú	34. GUR	35. ia
36. um	37. e	38. qa	39. as	40. GU_4
41. ni	42. en	43. ta	44. ra	45. LÚ
46. be	47. GIŠ	48. ša	49. ik	50. GAL

51. wa	52. sa	53. še	54. ak	55. ri

56. te	57. iš	58. IKU	59. na	60. ṣi

61. É	62. up	63. DINGIR	64. nu	65. šum

66. al	67. ti	68. li	69. nam	70. tim

71. pu	72. at	73. it	74. šu	75. q̣á

ANSWERS

1.	2.	3.	4.	5.
6.	7.	8.	9.	10.
11.	12.	13.	14.	15.
16.	17.	18.	19.	20.
21.	22.	23.	24.	25.
26.	27.	28.	29.	30.
31.	32.	33.	34.	35.
36.	37.	38.	39.	40.
41.	42.	43.	44.	45.
46.	47.	48.	49.	50.
51.	52.	53.	54.	55.
56.	57.	58.	59.	60.
61.	62.	63.	64.	65.
66.	67.	68.	69.	70.
71.	72.	73.	74.	75.

If you missed one sign, practice it here. If you missed more than one, go back to the places where those signs were first presented and work through the sections on each again. Then go on to Section Six.

Sign ______ :

Section Six

384 The next sign is ŠÀ, , a logogram for 'heart', translated by Akkadian libbu. It is UTU, , with two following verticals. Try it: , , .

ŠÀ	ŠÀ	ŠÀ	ŠÀ	ŠÀ
ŠÀ	ŠÀ	ŠÀ	ŠÀ	ŠÀ

(repeated)

Transliterate:

= ____ ____ ____ ____

= ____ ____

i-na ŠÀ LÚ 'in a man's heart'

ŠÀ.TAM= šatammu '(an official)'

Put into cuneiform:

i-na ŠÀ É 'inside a house'

dŠÀ.ZU '(a name for the god Marduk)'

Practice ŠÀ until you feel sure of it. Keep it distinct in your mind from UTU and wa.

ŠÀ	UTU	ŠÀ	wa	ŠÀ
ŠÀ	wa	ŠÀ	UTU	ŠÀ

repeated

396 The next sign is ḫi, [cuneiform]. It is the last element of gi, [cuneiform]. Try it:

ḫi	ḫi	ḫi	ḫi	ḫi
ḫi	ḫi	ḫi	ḫi	ḫi

[cuneiform] repeated

Transliterate:

[cuneiform] = ____ ____ ____

[cuneiform] = ____ ____ ____ ____

i-ḫi-iz 'mountings of'

na-ḫi-ra-šu 'his nostril' (accusative)

Put into cuneiform:

É ḫi-la-an-ni 'type of palace'

sa-ḫi-ru 'turning'

[cuneiform]

[cuneiform]

Practice ḫi to keep it distinct in your mind from the similar sign še.

ḫi	še	ḫi	še	ḫi
ḫi	ḫi	ḫi	ḫi	ḫi

[cuneiform]

repeated

398 The next sign is ah̯, ih̯, eh̯, uh̯, [cuneiform]. It begins with h̯i, [cuneiform], [cuneiform]. Try it:

ah̯	ah̯	ah̯	ah̯	ah̯
ah̯	ah̯	ah̯	ah̯	ah̯

[cuneiform] repeated

Transliterate:

[cuneiform] = ______ ______ ______

[cuneiform] = ______ ______ ______

ih̯-šu-uh̯ 'he desired'

mu-uh̯-h̯u 'front'

Put into cuneiform:

ah̯-h̯i 'of brothers'

pu-uh̯-h̯u-ru 'to assemble'

[cuneiform]

Practice ah̯ until you feel sure of it.

ah̯	ah̯	ah̯	ah̯	ah̯
ah̯	ah̯	ah̯	ah̯	ah̯

[cuneiform] repeated

399 The next sign is im, em, [cuneiform] . It is the reverse of gi, [cuneiform] . Try it:

im	im	im	im	im
im	im	im	im	im

Transliterate:

[cuneiform] = _____ _____ _____

[cuneiform] = _____ _____ _____ _____

[cuneiform] repeated

Put into cuneiform:

ni-iš i-li-im 'oath of a god'

im-ma-ru 'they see'

im-du-um 'support'

e im-ra-aṣ 'let him not worry'

Practice im and keep it distinct in your mind from gi.

im	gi	im	gi	im
im	im	im	im	im

[cuneiform]

[cuneiform] repeated

406 The next sign is kam, [cuneiform]. It is used as a syllabic value, but it is also used as a logogram, read KAM, to indicate that the preceding sign is an ordinal number. The logographic use will be encountered later when we have learned some number signs. Kam is ḫi, [cuneiform], plus be, [cuneiform]. Try it: [cuneiform], [cuneiform], [cuneiform].

kam	kam	kam	kam	kam
kam	kam	kam	kam	kam

[cuneiform] repeated

Transliterate:

[cuneiform] = ____ ____ ____ ____

[cuneiform] = ____ ____ ____

kam-kam-ma-tu '(kind of ring)'

na-kam-tum 'storehouse'

Put into cuneiform:

kam-mu '(a fungus)'

kam-ma-al šar-ru-ti 'adversary(?) of kingship'

[cuneiform]

Practice kam until you feel sure of it. Keep it distinct in your mind from aḫ.

kam	aḫ	kam	aḫ	kam
kam	kam	kam	kam	kam

[cuneiform] repeated

411 The next sign is the logogram for the number 10, 𒌋 , read U in Sumerian and <u>ešir</u> in Akkadian. It is merely a single diagonal wedge. Try it:

U	U	U	U	U
U	U	U	U	U

Transliterate:

= _____ _____ _____

= _____ _____ _____

𒌋 repeated

Put into cuneiform:

É 10-KAM 'tenth house'

<u>ša-at-tum</u> 10-KAM 'tenth year'

U_4 10-KAM '10th day'
LÚ 10-KAM '10th man'

Practice U until you feel sure of it.

U	U	U	U	U
U	U	U	U	U

𒌋 repeated

427 The next sign is mi, [cuneiform], which begins with U. Try it: [cuneiform], [cuneiform], [cuneiform].

mi	mi	mi	mi	mi
mi	mi	mi	mi	mi

Transliterate:

[cuneiform] = ____ ____ ____

[cuneiform] = ____ ____ ____ ____

[cuneiform] repeated

Put into cuneiform:

*mi-gi-ir-ka 'your consent'

e-mi-id 'it is standing'

um-mi-šu 'of his mother'

mi-iṣ-ru-um 'border'

Practice mi until you feel sure of it.

mi	mi	mi	mi	mi
mi	mi	mi	mi	mi

[cuneiform]

[cuneiform] repeated

433 The next sign is nim, [cuneiform], which starts like mi, [cuneiform], but ends in a diagonal wedge and a vertical wedge. Try it: [cuneiform], [cuneiform], [cuneiform].

nim	nim	nim	nim	nim
nim	nim	nim	nim	nim

[cuneiform] repeated

Transliterate:

[cuneiform] = ____ ____

[cuneiform] = ____ ____ ____ ____ ____

nim-ru 'leopard'

Put into cuneiform:

da-na-nim 'of strength'

iš-pu-ru-nim 'they wrote to me'

nim-gal-li du-ri '(a siege device)'

[cuneiform]

Practice nim until you feel sure of it. Be sure to keep it separate in your mind from mi.

nim	mi	nim	mi	nim
nim	nim	nim	nim	nim

[cuneiform] repeated

435 The next sign is lam, [cuneiform] , which is distinguished from nim, [cuneiform] , by having one more vertical at the end. Try it: [cuneiform] , [cuneiform] , [cuneiform] .

lam	lam	lam	lam	lam
lam	lam	lam	lam	lam

[cuneiform] repeated

Transliterate:

[cuneiform] = _____ _____ _____

[cuneiform] = _____ _____ _____ _____

ṣi-il-lam 'shadow' (accusative)

Put into cuneiform:

i-lam-ma-du 'he understands' (subjunctive)

GIŠ lam-mu 'almond tree'

*ša-lam dUTU 'sunset'

[cuneiform]

Practice lam until you feel sure of it. Be sure to keep it distinct in your mind from nim.

lam	nim	lam	nim	lam
lam	lam	lam	lam	lam

[cuneiform] repeated

437 The next sign is AMAR, , a logogram for 'calf', with the Akkadian translation būru. It resembles mi, , but has two diagonal wedges at the end. Try it: , , .

AMAR	AMAR	AMAR	AMAR	AMAR
AMAR	AMAR	AMAR	AMAR	AMAR

Transliterate: = _____ _____

= _____ _____

repeated

Put into cuneiform:

^{d}AMAR.UTU=Marduk (a god)

AMAR.^{d}EN.ZU=Būr-Sîn (a personal name)

AMAR-ni 'our calf'

AMAR.GA= būr šizbi 'suckling' (literally 'calf of milk')

Practice AMAR until you feel sure of it. Be sure not to confuse it with mi.

AMAR	mi	AMAR	mi	AMAR
AMAR	AMAR	AMAR	AMAR	AMAR

---

repeated

441 The next sign is ul, [cuneiform], which is GU_4, [cuneiform], preceded by U, [cuneiform]. Try it: [cuneiform], [cuneiform], [cuneiform].

ul	ul	ul	ul	ul
ul	ul	ul	ul	ul

[cuneiform] repeated

Transliterate:

[cuneiform] = ____ ____ ____

[cuneiform] = ____ ____

i-pu-ul 'he answered'
ul-tu 'from'

Put into cuneiform:

pu-ul-ḫi-tum 'being fearful'

ḫu-ul-la-nu '(a blanket)'

[cuneiform]

Practice ul until you are sure of it. Be sure to keep it distinct in your mind from GU_4.

ul	GU_4	ul	GU_4	ul
ul	ul	ul	ul	ul

[cuneiform] repeated

449 The next sign is <u>ši</u>, [cuneiform sign], which also starts with U. Try it: [cuneiform], [cuneiform], [cuneiform].

ši	ši	ši	ši	ši
ši	ši	ši	ši	ši

[cuneiform] repeated

Transliterate:

[cuneiform] = _____ _____ _____

[cuneiform] = _____ _____ _____ _____

<u>ši-im-tu</u> 'fate'

<u>ši-ḫi-it-tum</u> '(a plant)'

Put into cuneiform:

<u>ka-ši-id</u> 'it is conquered'

<u>i-na-aš-ši</u> 'he lifts'

[cuneiform]

[cuneiform]

Practice <u>ši</u> until you feel sure of it and can distinguish it from <u>wa</u>.

ši	wa	ši	wa	ši
ši	ši	ši	ši	ši

[cuneiform] repeated

451 The next sign is ar, [cuneiform], which is ši, [cuneiform], plus ri, [cuneiform]. Try it:

ar	ar	ar	ar	ar
ar	ar	ar	ar	ar

Transliterate:

[cuneiform] = ____ ____

[cuneiform] = ____ ____ ____ ____

[cuneiform] repeated

Put into cuneiform:

ša-ar ma-ti 'king of the land'

ar-na-ba-tim 'hares'

ar-nu 'sin'

ma-ar-ti-ka 'of your daughter'

Practice ar until you feel sure of it.

ar	ar	ar	ar	ar
ar	ar	ar	ar	ar

[cuneiform]

[cuneiform] repeated

455 The next sign is ù, [cuneiform], which is ši, [cuneiform], plus lu, [cuneiform], a sign to be learned later. This sign is frequently used for the word u 'and'. Try it: [cuneiform], [cuneiform], [cuneiform].

ù	ù	ù	ù	ù
ù	ù	ù	ù	ù

[cuneiform] repeated

Transliterate:

[cuneiform]

______ ______ ______ ______ ______ ______

ša-ar-ru ù ru-bu 'king and noble'

Put into cuneiform:

um-mu ù DUMU 'mother and son'

[cuneiform]

Practice ù until you feel sure of it.

ù	ù	ù	ù	ù
ù	ù	ù	ù	ù

[cuneiform] repeated

457 The next sign is di, , composed of U, , plus a vertical, plus pa, .

Try it: , , .

di	di	di	di	di
di	di	di	di	di

Put into cuneiform:

ti-di 'you know' di-im-tu 'tower'

repeated

Transliterate:

= ______ ______

= ______ ______ ______ ______

Practice di until you feel sure of it.

di	di	di	di	di
di	di	di	di	di

di-nu 'legal decision'

wa-ar-di-šu 'of his slave'

On the next pages is a quiz on all the signs studied so far.

repeated

Section Six

QUIZ

1. ta	2. qa	3. ŠÀ	4. pa	5. lam	6. be
7. tu	8. ab	9. ni	10. ṣi	11. aḫ	12. il
13. aš	14. uk	15. kum	16. iš	17. it	18. ti
19. te	20. ši	21. ak	22. šum	23. li	24. ḫi
25. ru	26. ba	27. ik	28. na	29. mi	30. GAL
31. GIŠ	32. um	33. mu	34. ri	35. UTU	36. ú
37. DINGIR	38. en	39. ul	40. e	41. šu	42. at
43. qá	44. GU_4	45. ù	46. ar	47. É	48. i
49. da	50. pu	51. LÚ	52. la	53. ma	54. im

55. bí	56. si	57. bi	58. GUR	59. ša	60. di
61. še	62. in	63. ka	64. nam	65. nu	66. ra
67. zi	68. ḫu	69. gi	70. al	71.DUMU	72. uš
73. am	74. IKU	75. nim	76. sa	77. tim	78. U
79. SAG	80. as	81. zu	82.AMAR	83. wa	84. up
85. tum	86. du	87. ia	88. kam	89. šar	90. ir

ANSWERS

1.	2.	3.	4.	5.	6.
7.	8.	9.	10.	11.	12.
13.	14.	15.	16.	17.	18.
19.	20.	21.	22.	23.	24.
25.	26.	27.	28.	29.	30.
31.	32.	33.	34.	35.	36.
37.	38.	39.	40.	41.	42.
43.	44.	45.	46.	47.	48.
49.	50.	51.	52.	53.	54.
55.	56.	57.	58.	59.	60.
61.	62.	63.	64.	65.	66.
67.	68.	69.	70.	71.	72.
73.	74.	75.	76.	77.	78.
79.	80.	81.	82.	83.	84.
85.	86.	87.	88.	89.	90.

If you missed one sign, practice it here. If you missed more than one, go back to the places where the signs were first presented and work again through those parts. Then go on to Section Seven.

Sign ______ :

Section Seven

461 The next sign is ki, [cuneiform], consisting of U, [cuneiform], plus ku, [cuneiform], a sign to be learned later. Try it: [cuneiform], [cuneiform], [cuneiform].

ki	ki	ki	ki	ki
ki	ki	ki	ki	ki

Transliterate:

[cuneiform] = ____ ____ ____ ____

[cuneiform] = ____ ____ ____

[cuneiform] repeated

Put into cuneiform:

ki-sa-al-li 'of a vestibule'

ki-ma 'like'

ki-la-la-an 'both'

ki-iṣ-ru 'knot'

Practice ki to keep it separate in your mind from di.

ki	di	ki	di	ki
ki	ki	ki	ki	ki

[cuneiform]

[cuneiform]

[cuneiform]

repeated

468 The next sign is KÙ, , a logogram for 'pure', translated by Akkadian ellu. Try it: , , .

KÙ	KÙ	KÙ	KÙ	KÙ
KÙ	KÙ	KÙ	KÙ	KÙ

Transliterate: = _____ _____

= _____ _____ _____

repeated

Put into cuneiform:

KÙ.GI=hurāṣu 'gold' KÙ.IM.BA=butuqqû 'loss'

KÙ.BABBAR= kaspu 'silver'
LÚ.KÙ.ZU= emqu 'wise man'

Practice KÙ until you feel sure of it.

KÙ	KÙ	KÙ	KÙ	KÙ
KÙ	KÙ	KÙ	KÙ	KÙ

---

repeated

472 The next sign, <u>eš</u>, 𒌍 , is simply three U's, 𒌋 . Try it:

eš	eš	eš	eš	eš
eš	eš	eš	eš	eš

Transliterate: 𒌍 𒋗 = ____ ____

𒄿 𒌍 = ____ ____

𒌍 repeated

Put into cuneiform:

<u>eš-re-ti-šu</u> 'of his tenth'

<u>te-eš-mu-um</u> 'acceptance'

<u>eš-šu</u> 'new'

<u>e-eš</u> 'where?'

Practice <u>eš</u> until you feel sure of it.

eš	eš	eš	eš	eš
eš	eš	eš	eš	eš

𒌍 𒊑 𒋾 𒋗

𒋼 𒌍 𒈬 𒌝

𒌍 repeated

480 The next sign is DIŠ, , a logogram for the number 1, Akkadian <u>ištēn</u>. It is not to be confused with <u>aš</u>, , which also consists of a single wedge. Try it:

DIŠ	DIŠ	DIŠ	DIŠ	DIŠ
DIŠ	DIŠ	DIŠ	DIŠ	DIŠ

Transliterate:

= ______ ______ ______

= ______ ______ ______

repeated

Put into cuneiform:

É 1-KAM
'the first house'

11 (eleven) = <u>ištēnešret</u>
= <u>10 + 1</u>

LÚ 1-KAM
'the first man'

U_4 1-KAM
'the first day'

Practice DIŠ until you feel sure of it. Be sure to keep it distinct in your mind from <u>aš</u>.

DIŠ	DIŠ	DIŠ	DIŠ	DIŠ
DIŠ	aš	DIŠ	aš	DIŠ

---

repeated

532 The next sign is me, 𒈨 , which is a vertical plus aš, 𒀸 . Try it:

me	me	me	me	me
me	me	me	me	me

Transliterate:

𒌍 𒈨 𒆪 = _____ _____ _____

𒈨 𒇷 𒅎 𒈪 = _____ _____ _____ _____

𒈨

repeated

Put into cuneiform:

Iš-me-^{d}EN.ZU

'the god Sin heard' (a personal name)

ka-ar-me 'ruins'

eš-me-kum

'(a stone)'

me-li-im-mi

'of a fearsome look'

Practice me.

me	me	me	me	me
me	me	me	me	me

𒅖 𒈨 𒆪

𒅎 𒈪

𒅗 𒅈 𒈨

𒈨

repeated

533 The next sign is MEŠ, , a logogram indicating the plural. It is a ligature of <u>me</u>, , and <u>eš</u>, . Try it: , , .

MEŠ	MEŠ	MEŠ	MEŠ	MEŠ
MEŠ	MEŠ	MEŠ	MEŠ	MEŠ

Transliterate: = ____ ____

= ____ ____

repeated

Put into cuneiform:

AMAR.MEŠ=<u>būrū</u> 'calves'

U$_4$.MEŠ=<u>ūmū</u> 'days'

É.MEŠ= <u>bītātu</u> 'houses'

LÚ.MEŠ= <u>awīlū</u> 'men'

Practice MEŠ until you feel sure of it. Be sure to keep it distinct in your mind from <u>me</u>.

MEŠ	me	MEŠ	me	MEŠ
MEŠ	MEŠ	MEŠ	MEŠ	MEŠ

---

repeated

535 The next sign, which begins like me, is ib, ip, . Try it: , , .

ib	ib	ib	ib	ib
ib	ib	ib	ib	ib

Transliterate:

= _____ _____ _____

= _____ _____ _____

repeated

Put into cuneiform:

ip-ḫu-ru 'they assembled'

ip-li-šu-nu 'of their compensation payment'

li-ib-ni 'may he build'

ṣi-ib-tu 'interest'

Practice ib until you feel sure of it.

ib	ib	ib	ib	ib
ib	ib	ib	ib	ib

---

repeated

536 The next sign is <u>ku</u>, , which is the second element in <u>ki</u>, . Try it:

ku	ku	ku	ku	ku
ku	ku	ku	ku	ku

Transliterate:

= _____ _____

= _____ _____ _____

repeated

Put into cuneiform:

<u>ar-ku</u> 'long' <u>ku-uk-ru</u> '(a plant)'

<u>da-ku</u>
'to kill'
<u>il-li-ku</u>
'they went'

Practice <u>ku</u> until you feel sure of it.

ku	ku	ku	ku	ku
ku	ku	ku	ku	ku

---

repeated

537 The next sign is lu, , which is the second element in ù, . It is the same as ku but with one more vertical following. Try it:

lu	lu	lu	lu	lu
lu	lu	lu	lu	lu

Transliterate:

= ____ ____ ____

= ____ ____ ____

repeated

Put into cuneiform:

wa-ba-lu 'to carry'

lu-ku-ul 'let me eat'

aš-lu-uk-ka-tu 'storehouse'

be-lu 'lord'

Practice lu to keep it distinct in your mind from ku.

lu	ku	lu	ku	lu
lu	lu	lu	lu	lu

---

repeated

554 The next sign is SAL, [cuneiform], a logogram for 'woman', Akkadian <u>sinništu</u>. It is used as a determinative before women's personal and professional names. It also has the reading GEME 'female slave' with the Akkadian translation <u>amtu</u>. SAL begins like the middle element in <u>up</u>, [cuneiform], and has a horizontal at the end.

Try it: [cuneiform], [cuneiform], [cuneiform].

SAL	SAL	SAL	SAL	SAL
SAL	SAL	SAL	SAL	SAL

[cuneiform] repeated

Transliterate:

[cuneiform] = ____ ____ ____ ____

[cuneiform] = ____ ____ ____ ____

SAL<u>ši-ib-tu</u> 'female witness'

SAL<u>ša-il-tu</u> 'female dream interpreter'

Put into cuneiform:

DUMU.SAL = mārtu 'daughter'		1 SAG.GEME 'one (head) female slave'		

Practice SAL until you feel sure of it.

SAL	SAL	SAL	SAL	SAL
SAL	SAL	SAL	SAL	SAL

On the next pages is a quiz on all the signs studied so far.

repeated

Section Seven

QUIZ

1. wa	2. aš	3. as	4. at	5. ak

6. te	7. mi	8. GU_4	9. si	10. kam

11. GAL	12. zi	13. zu	14. kum	15. qa

16. nim	17. up	18. ti	19. ši	20. LÚ

21. ba	22. ia	23. UTU	24. al	25. be

26. li	27. ri	28. bí	29. it	30. lu

31. du	32. ḫi	33. eš	34. ib	35. GUR

36. ṣi	37. ma	38. en	39. pu	40. ar

41. SAG	42. uš	43. DINGIR	44. pa	45. il

46. tum	47. ku	48. mu	49. ik	50. ul

51. di	52.DUMU	53. um	54. qá	55. GIŠ
56. tim	57. ni	58. ù	59. aḫ	60. tu
61. am	62. me	63. U	64. ir	65. ru
66. KÙ	67. iš	68. ki	69. nu	70. ša
71. in	72. IKU	73. e	74. É	75. sa
76. ú	77. da	78. i	79. šu	80. DIŠ
81. nam	82. gi	83. na	84. ka	85. ta
86. im	87. ra	88.AMAR	89. šum	90. uk
91. SAL	92. MEŠ	93. ab	94. še	95. lam
96. ḫu	97. la	98. bi	99. šar	100. ŠÀ

ANSWERS

1.	2.	3.	4.	5.
6.	7.	8.	9.	10.
11.	12.	13.	14.	15.
16.	17.	18.	19.	20.
21.	22.	23.	24.	25.
26.	27.	28.	29.	30.
31.	32.	33.	34.	35.
36.	37.	38.	39.	40.
41.	42.	43.	44.	45.
46.	47.	48.	49.	50.
51.	52.	53.	54.	55.
56.	57.	58.	59.	60.
61.	62.	63.	64.	65.
66.	67.	68.	69.	70.
71.	72.	73.	74.	75.
76.	77.	78.	79.	80.
81.	82.	83.	84.	85.
86.	87.	88.	89.	90.
91.	92.	93.	94.	95.
96.	97.	98.	99.	100.

If you missed one sign, practice it here. If you missed more than one, return to the sections where the signs were first introduced and work again through them.

Sign _______ :

Section Eight

556 The next sign is nin, , which is SAL, , plus ma, . As a logogram read NIN the sign means 'lady' and is translated by Akkadian beltu. Try it: , , .

nin	nin	nin	nin	nin
nin	nin	nin	nin	nin

Transliterate:

= _____ _____ _____

= _____ _____ _____ _____

repeated

Put into cuneiform:

^{d}NIN.GAL-um-mi
'the goddess Ningal is my mother'
(a personal name)

nin-da-nu 'measuring rod'

ša-nin-šu 'his equal'

la te-nin-ni 'do not punish me'

Practice nin until you feel sure of it. Keep it distinct in your mind from SAL.

nin	SAL	nin	SAL	nin
nin	nin	nin	nin	nin

repeated

557 The next sign is dam, [cuneiform], which is exactly the same as nin, [cuneiform], except for one additional horizontal wedge in the ma element. As a logogram it is read DAM and means 'spouse' with the Akkadian equivalents mutu 'husband' and aššatu 'wife'. Try it: [cuneiform], [cuneiform], [cuneiform].

dam	dam	dam	dam	dam
dam	dam	dam	dam	dam

[cuneiform] repeated

Transliterate:

[cuneiform] = ____ ____ ____ ____

[cuneiform] = ____ ____ ____

dam-qa i-ni 'with beautiful (?) eyes'

ú-ri-dam 'he came down'

Put into cuneiform:

dam-qá-am 'fine' (accusative)

dam-tam iš-pu-uk 'he heaped up destruction(?)'

Practice dam until you feel sure of it. Be sure to keep it distinct in your mind from nin.

dam	nin	dam	nin	dam
dam	dam	dam	dam	dam

---

repeated

564 The next sign is el, [cuneiform], composed of SAL's first element, plus si plus a vertical, written [cuneiform], [cuneiform], [cuneiform]. Try it:

el	el	el	el	el
el	el	el	el	el

Transliterate:

[cuneiform] = ____ ____ ____

[cuneiform] = ____ ____ ____

[cuneiform] repeated

Put into cuneiform:

el-ṣi-iš 'joyfully'

el-bi-iš 'proudly'

el-me-šu '(a stone)'

el-li-bu '(a plant)'

Practice el until you feel sure of it.

el	el	el	el	el
el	el	el	el	el

[cuneiform]

[cuneiform]

[cuneiform] repeated

565 The next sign is lum, , which begins like SAL, , but ends in four horizontals. Try it: , , .

lum	lum	lum	lum	lum
lum	lum	lum	lum	lum

repeated

Transliterate:

= ___ ___ ___ ___

= ___ ___ ___ ___

Put into cuneiform:

ba-la-lum 'to mix'

šu-lum-ki 'your(feminine) well-being'

šu-uk-lu-lum 'to complete'

gi-mi-il-lum 'act of kindness'

Practice lum and el.

lum	el	lum	el	lum
lum	lum	lum	lum	lum

---

repeated

570 The next sign is MIN, [cuneiform] , a logogram for the number 2 , translated by Akkadian <u>šina</u>. It is simply two DIŠ signs, [cuneiform] . Try it:

MIN	MIN	MIN	MIN	MIN
MIN	MIN	MIN	MIN	MIN

[cuneiform] repeated

Transliterate:

[cuneiform] = ____ ____ ____

[cuneiform] = ____ ____ ____ ____

É 2-KAM 'second house'

SAG.AMAR 2-KAM 'second (head of) calf'

Put into cuneiform:

U_4 12(=10+2)-KAM 'twelfth day'

LÚ 12-KAM 'twelfth man'

[cuneiform]

[cuneiform]

Practice MIN until you feel sure of it.

MIN	MIN	MIN	MIN	MIN
MIN	MIN	MIN	MIN	MIN

[cuneiform] repeated

575 The next sign is ur, , which is the opposite of ib, . Ib has the element me, , first. Try ur.

ur	ur	ur	ur	ur
ur	ur	ur	ur	ur

Transliterate:

= ___ ___ ___

= ___ ___ ___

(margin: repeated)

Put into cuneiform:

pu-zu-ur 'secret of'

du-ur 'wall of'

im-ḫu-ur 'he received'

ur-ba-ti 'of reed'

Practice ur until you feel sure of it. Keep it distinct in your mind from ib.

ur	ib	ur	ib	ur
ur	ur	ur	ur	ur

---

repeated

579 The next sign is a, 𒀀 , the final element in e, 𒂊 . Try it:

a	a	a	a	a
a	a	a	a	a

𒀀 repeated

Transliterate:

𒀀 𒈠 𒌈 = _____ _____ _____

𒀀 𒁲 = _____ _____

a-ma-tum 'word'

a-di 'until'

Put into cuneiform:

a-ka-lu 'to eat'

a-pu-ul 'I replied'

𒀀 𒅗 𒇻

𒀀 𒁍 𒌌

Practice a until you feel sure of it.

a	a	a	a	a
a	a	a	a	a

𒀀 repeated

586 The next sign is <u>ṣa</u>, <u>za</u>, [cuneiform], which is the final inscribed element in <u>as</u>, [cuneiform]. Try it:

ṣa	ṣa	ṣa	ṣa	ṣa
ṣa	ṣa	ṣa	ṣa	ṣa

[cuneiform] repeated

Transliterate:

[cuneiform] = ____ ____ ____

[cuneiform] = ____ ____ ____

ṣa-ra-pu 'to burn'

ṣa-la-mi 'of becoming dark'

Put into cuneiform:

<u>pa-ṣa-du</u> 'to cut'

<u>i-ṣa-a-a-ad</u> 'he makes his rounds'

[cuneiform]

Practice <u>ṣa</u> until you feel sure of it. Be sure to keep it distinct in your mind from <u>a</u>.

ṣa	a	ṣa	a	ṣa
ṣa	ṣa	ṣa	ṣa	ṣa

[cuneiform] repeated

589 The next sign is ḫa, , which is ṣa, , plus U, . Try it:

ḫa	ḫa	ḫa	ḫa	ḫa
ḫa	ḫa	ḫa	ḫa	ḫa

Transliterate:

= ____ ____ ____

= ____ ____ ____ ____

repeated

Put into cuneiform:

ḫa-aḫ-ḫu 'spittle'

ḫa-du-ú 'to be happy'

ḫa-ru-bu 'carob'

te-er-ḫa-at 'bride price of'

Practice ḫa until you feel sure of it. Be sure to keep it distinct in your mind from ṣa.

ḫa	ṣa	ḫa	ṣa	ḫa
ḫa	ḫa	ḫa	ḫa	ḫa

---

repeated

595 The next sign is GÍN, [cuneiform], a logogram for 'sheqel', a small measure of weight equivalent to about 8.33 grams in some periods; the Akkadian translation is <u>šiqlu</u>. Try it: [cuneiform], [cuneiform], [cuneiform]. [cuneiform], [cuneiform].

GÍN	GÍN	GÍN	GÍN	GÍN
GÍN	GÍN	GÍN	GÍN	GÍN

[cuneiform] repeated

Transliterate:

[cuneiform] = _____ _____ _____ _____

[cuneiform] = _____ _____ _____ _____

Put into cuneiform:

<u>i-na</u> 1 GÍN.GAL 'in one large sheqel'

2 GÍN <u>za-ba-lum</u> '2 sheqels of (a resin)'

1 GÍN KÙ.BABBAR '1 sheqel silver'

10 GÍN KÙ.GI '10 sheqels gold'

Practice GÍN until you feel sure of it.

GÍN	GÍN	GÍN	GÍN	GÍN
GÍN	GÍN	GÍN	GÍN	GÍN

[cuneiform]

[cuneiform] repeated

You have now studied the basic signs of the cuneiform system. If you have learned them, you may be justly proud of your achievement.

You will find that if you read texts from other periods than the Old Babylonian, you will encounter signs which you have not studied here and which are more frequent than some of those that you did already learn. And the signs you already know will occur with other readings than the ones that you studied. What you have to do now is to learn these other values for the signs you know and to learn other signs which are popular in other periods.

If the active method of sign learning has proven useful for you, you should try systematically to learn to recognize and to produce signs that occur in your reading or which your teacher recommends.

On the following pages is a quiz over all the basic signs.

FINAL QUIZ

1. ak	2. qá	3. IKU	4. ib	5. ia
6. GIŠ	7. tum	8. lum	9. uk	10.AMAR
11. tu	12. da	13. at	14. el	15. ba
16. kam	17. mi	18. zi	19. ni	20. GUR
21. te	22. SAL	23. e	24. la	25.DINGIR
26. MIN	27. in	28. bi	29. im	30. pa
31. si	32. lam	33. ḫa	34. GAL	35. nu
36. ŠÀ	37. ur	38. mu	39. É	40. ar
41. šum	42. zu	43. šar	44. dam	45. ḫu
46. ul	47. du	48. am	49. ra	50. gi
51. me	52. U	53. up	54. na	55. as

56. pu	57. lu	58. qa	59. bí	60. šu
61. DUMU	62. a	63. ka	64. al	65. ir
66. ru	67. tim	68. GÍN	69. UTU	70. ab
71. ša	72. GU_4	73. i	74. ù	75. DIŠ
76. ma	77. nam	78. di	79. ṣa	80. uš
81. ki	82. aš	83. ḫi	84. ta	85. ku
86. SAG	87. it	88. LÚ	89. KÙ	90. en
91. ri	92. nim	93. MEŠ	94. aḫ	95. ik
96. um	97. il	98. wa	99. be	100. nin
101. ši	102. sa	103. eš	104. li	105. kum
106. še	107. ú	108. ṣi	109. iš	110. ti

ANSWERS

1.	2.	3.	4.	5.
6.	7.	8.	9.	10.
11.	12.	13.	14.	15.
16.	17.	18.	19.	20.
21.	22.	23.	24.	25.
26.	27.	28.	29.	30.
31.	32.	33.	34.	35.
36.	37.	38.	39.	40.
41.	42.	43.	44.	45.
46.	47.	48.	49.	50.
51.	52.	53.	54.	55.
56.	57.	58.	59.	60.
61.	62.	63.	64.	65.
66.	67.	68.	69.	70.
71.	72.	73.	74.	75.
76.	77.	78.	79.	80.
81.	82.	83.	84.	85.
86.	87.	88.	89.	90.
91.	92.	93.	94.	95.
96.	97.	98.	99.	100.
101.	102.	103.	104.	105.
106.	107.	108.	109.	110.

If you missed one sign, practice it here. If you missed more than one, go back to the places where the signs were first presented and work again through those parts.

Sign ______ :

Alphabetic List of Values

Only values taught within this workbook are listed here. The number to the right of the sign indicates the page number of the workbook where the sign was first presented. Signs for numbers are grouped at the end of this list.

a	129
ab	36
ad	45
ag	26
aḫ	92
ak	26
al	65
am	49
AMAR	99
an	5
ap	36
aq	26
ar	102
as	38
aṣ	38
aš	2
at	45
az	38
ba	3
BABBAR	84
be	13
bi	59
bí	50
bu	82
da	76
dam	123
di	104
DINGIR	5
DIŠ	111
du	55
DUMU	44
e	67
É	72
eḫ	92
el	125
em	93
en	27
er	61
eš	110
ga	71
GAL, gal	78
GEME	117
gi	23
GÍN	132
GIŠ	63
GU_4	64
GUR	30
ḫa	131
ḫi	91
ḫu	19
i	42
ia	43
ib	114
id	75
iḫ	92
ik	21
IKU	29
il	54
im	93
in	47
ip	114
iq	21
ir	61
is	63
iṣ	63
iš	58
it, iṭ	75
iz	63
ka	6
kam	94
KAM	94
ki	108
ku	115
KÙ	109
kum	51
la	7
lam	98
li	9
lu	116
LÚ	74
lum	126
ma	77
me	112

Reading	No.
MEŠ	113
mi	96
MIN	127
mu	10
na	14
nam	20
ne	50
ni	60
nim	97
nin	122
nu	16
pa	62
pi	86
pu	82
qa	11
qá	71
qum, qu	51
ra	73
re	24
ri	24
ru	12
sa	28
SAG	32
SAL	117
si	31
ṣa	130
ṣi	46
ša	79
ŠÀ	90
šar	48
še	81
ši	101

Reading	No.
šu	80
šum	33
ta	41
tam	84
te	83
ti	15
tim	25
tu	8
tum	56
U	95
ú	68
ù	103
U_4	84
ub	66
ud	84
ug	37
uḫ	92
uk	37
ul	100
um	40
up	66
uq	37
ur	128
uš	57
ut	84
UTU	84
wa	86
wi	86
wu	86
za	130
zi	22
zu	4

<u>Numbers</u>

Number	No.
1	111
	29
2	127
10	95

List of Signs

Only values taught within this workbook are listed; the number to the right indicates the page number of the workbook where the sign was first presented.

aš,1 2,29
ba 3
zu 4
DINGIR, an 5
ka 6
la 7
tu 8
li 9
mu 10
qa 11
ru 12
be 13
na 14
ti 15
nu 16
ḫu 19
nam 20
ik,iq 21
zi 22
gi 23
ri,re 24
tim 25
ak,aq,ag 26
en 27
sa 28
IKU 29
GUR 30
si 31
SAG 32

šum 33
ab,ab 36
uk,uq,ug 37
as,az,aṣ 38
um 40
ta 41
i 42
ia 43
DUMU 44
at,ad 45
ṣi 46
in 47
šar 48
am 49
bí,ne 50
kum,qum,qu 51
il 54
du 55
tum 56
uš 57
iš 58
bi 59
ni 60
ir,er 61
pa 62
GIŠ, is,iz,iṣ 63
GU_4 64
al 65
up,ub 66

e 67
ú 68
qá,ga 71
É 72
ra 73
LÚ 74
it,iṭ,id 75
da 76
ma 77
GAL,gal 78
ša 79
šu 80
še 81
pu,bu 82
te 83
UTU,BABBAR, U_4,tam,ut, ud 84
wa,wi,wu, pi 86
ŠÀ 90
ḫi 91
aḫ,iḫ, eḫ,uḫ 92
im,em 93
kam,KAM 94
U,10 95
mi 96
nim 97
lam 98
AMAR 99

ul 100
ši 101
ar 102
ù 103
di 104
ki 108
KÙ 109
eš 110
DIŠ,1 111
me 112
MEŠ 113
ib,ip 114
ku 115
lu 116
SAL,GEME 117
nin,NIN 122
dam,DAM 123
el 125
lum 126
MIN,2 127
ur 128
a 129
ṣa,za 130
ḫa 131
GÍN 132